AMERICAN POETS PROJECT

The American Poets Project
is published with a gift in memory of
JAMES MERRILL

Poets of
World War II

harvey shapiro editor

AMERICAN POETS PROJECT

THE LIBRARY OF AMERICA

Some of the material in this volume is reprinted with permission of the holders of
copyright and publication rights. Acknowledgments are on pages 243–50.

The paper used in this publication meets the minimum requirements of the
American National Standard for Information Sciences—Permanence of Paper
for Printed Library materials, ANSI Z39.48—1984.

Design by Chip Kidd and Mark Melnick.
Frontispiece: Harvey Shapiro, April 1945.

Library of Congress Cataloging in Publication Data:
Poets of World War II / Harvey Shapiro, editor.
p. cm.— (American poets project ; 2)
Includes index.
1. American poetry—20th century. 2. World War, 1939–1945—Poetry. I Title:
Poets of World War 2. II Title: Poets of World War Two. III. Harvey Shapiro,
1924– IV. Series.
PS595 .W64 P65   2003
811.52080358— dc21
2002032125

10 9 8 7 6 5 4 3 2

Poets of
World War II

CONTENTS

INTRODUCTION

We were victorious, but the sight of dead bodies is scattered among these poems about World War II the way bodies were washed up on the shores of invasion beaches or left as markers along the trail to show the new infantrymen moving forward the face of death. And then, subliminally present, are those killed in the "clean war," the new war in the air, "who," as Howard Nemerov writes, "rarely bothered coming home to die."

Poems about any war share a subject that Simone Weil identified, in an essay about the *Iliad* that she wrote during World War II, as "force": "that *x* that turns anybody who is subjected to it into a *thing*. Exercised to the limit, it turns man into a thing in the most literal sense: it makes a corpse out of him." Or as Kenneth Koch puts it in "To World War Two":

> As machines make ice
> We made dead enemy soldiers.

Four hundred thousand Americans died in World War II. This is not a book of celebration, unless it is to celebrate man's ability, indeed his compulsion, to turn terror into art. It is, however, a book with a purpose: to demonstrate that the American poets of this war produced a body of work that has not yet been recognized for its clean and powerful eloquence. Comparisons can be odious, but common wisdom has it that the poets of World War I— Wilfred Owen, Robert Graves, Siegfried Sassoon, Edmund Blunden, Isaac Rosenberg—left us a monument and the poets of World War II did not. My hope is that readers of this book will come away convinced that is not the case.

There are continuities but mostly strong discontinuities between the English poets of that war and the American poets of this one. (The American poets of World War I—John Peale Bishop, E. E. Cummings, Archibald MacLeish, Alan Seeger—were too few to constitute a group.) In his classic anthology *Up the Line to Death: The War Poets 1914–18*, the English historian Brian Gardner singled out as a defining characteristic the poets' sense of themselves as a brotherhood. Even before the war, according to Gardner, they thought themselves a generation marked off for great things, and afterwards they remained a brotherhood of "those who were there." I find no evidence of a similar feeling among the American poets in these pages. But, of course, the English poets, officers all, belonged in a sense (with the exception of Rosenberg) to the same gentleman's club. The American poets, many of them enlisted men, did not.

There is sometimes a deliberate reaching back, an attempt to stand side by side with the poets of that first great war, as in Howard Nemerov's "A Fable of the War," a visionary poem that differs sharply from his poems about his experiences in aerial warfare. He sees himself in an unknown railroad station, under a frame of glass, with other soldiers who have recently disembarked.

> Suddenly, passing the known and unknown
> Bowed faces of my company, the sad
> And potent outfit of the armed, I see
> That we are dead. By stormless Acheron
> We stand easy, and the occasional moon
> Strikes terribly from steel and bone alike.

And the poem concludes:

> So, gentlemen—by greatcoat, cartridge belt
> And helmet held together for the time—
> In honorably enduring here we seek
> The second death. Until the worm shall bite
> To betray us, lean each man on his gun
> That the great work not falter but go on.

(The "So, gentlemen" gives it away.) Similarly in the infantry poems by Louis Simpson—the tight quatrains and the faux-naïve tone—I sense a linkage that goes back to Thomas Hardy's "Channel Firing," written on the eve of battle in 1914.

For the most part the Americans write in quite a different tone. Their poems are often bawdy, bitchy, irreverent. They do not glory in brotherhood and they do not, as a rule, find nobility in one another. Quite the contrary, they often dislike one another or dislike being put cheek by jowl alongside one another. If they are in the infantry, they bear no love for their officers (see Louis Simpson's "Carentan O Carentan"). To judge from my own experience, the fellow-feeling among soldiers in World War II often approached that suggested in Randall Jarrell's poem "O My Name It Is Sam Hall," which concerns three American prisoners and their guard in an army camp in the States. In the last stanza, the guard begins to sing "Sam Hall" and "They all stop and grin." It helps to know that song—and everyone in the army did—to appreciate the poem: "O my name it is Sam Hall / And I hate you one and all— / Yes, I hate you one and all, / God damn your eyes." Surprisingly, even those men in bomber crews, which were after all small, intensely coordinated units, could feel alien from one another (see Edward Field's graphic description of ditching a B-17 in the North Sea, "World War II"). If they write elegies, they write them mostly for themselves.

Nor do these poets sound the kind of sonorous note exemplified by John McCrae's "In Flanders Fields," the single poem from the First World War that everyone involved in the Second had grown up with—"To you from failing hands we throw / The torch; be yours to hold it high"—or by Rupert Brooke's "The Soldier:" "If I should die, think only this of me: / That there's some corner of a foreign field / That is forever England." (Of course, the tone of World War I poetry changed after the battles of the Somme in 1916, and the bitter poems of Owen, Sassoon, and Rudyard Kipling later in the war are closer to our own.)

The American poets of World War II wrote poems that are neither pious nor patriotic. This is as close as John Ciardi, one of the strongest poets here, gets to patriotism:

> I remember the United States of America
> As a flag-draped box with Arthur in it
> And six marines to bear it on their shoulders.

They viewed themselves as individuals caught in a giant machine that was so complex and far-flung the mind could not encompass it. They were astonished at the way their lives had been altered. As George Oppen writes in "Survival: Infantry": "And the world changed. / There had been trees and people, / Sidewalks and roads." They had a job to do, or a debt to pay to society, as one of them put it, and they went about doing it as best they could.

On the horizon in many of the poems in this collection, and sometimes much closer, is what changes everything—the airplane. The way trench warfare dominates the imagery of World War I, the fleets of bombers and the smoking cities dominate the imagery of World War II.

Out of that new war in the air came the most anthologized poem of the conflict, the only war poem most readers know, "The Death of the Ball Turret Gunner" by Randall Jarrell. Jarrell is unique among the poets in this collection. Already a well-known poet and professor, he enlisted in the Army Air Corps in 1942 but washed out of the flight part of his pilot's training program. Eventually, after further schooling, he became an instructor-trainer for navigators (part of a bombing crew) at Davis-Monthan Field in Tucson, Arizona. So this most famous poet of the war was an enlisted man in the Second Air Force, the training air force, and spent the war on the ground, Stateside. Some of his war poems are Stateside poems and come out of direct observation. He must have picked up the details for his poems of aerial combat over Europe and the Pacific by listening to the veterans who had returned from those theaters to instruct the young in the Second Air Force.

When I first read the concluding line of his famous five-line poem—"When I died they washed me out of the turret with a hose."—I was reminded abruptly of an incident from my aerial gunnery school training in Yuma, Arizona. We were outside, it was a bright, sunny day, and an instructor, a sergeant returned from flying his missions over Germany with the English-based 8th Air Force, was standing before a mock-up of a B-17 bomber, explaining the different positions a gunner might take in that plane (waist gun, tail gun, etc.). Then he came to the ball turret, which protrudes from the underbelly of the B-17, and said offhandedly, "Sometimes when they return from a mission, they have to wash him out of the turret with a hose." I made a note to myself to try hard to avoid that position. Jarrell may well have heard that line delivered just the way I did.

The war in the air is also covered vividly by the poets here who took part in it: Howard Nemerov, John Ciardi, William Meredith, Richard Hugo, James Dickey, and Edward Field. Hugo and Field let you know what it was like to crash in combat, Ciardi the many ways you can anticipate leaving this world on a mission. (Ciardi, who is now known chiefly for his Dante translation, should be better known for his war poems. They seem to have been written on the spot. I remember him at Yaddo, the artist's colony, in 1949—a big, swaggering man, he was called "the roller of big cigars"—improvising sonnets on the portraits that hung in the vestibule as we waited for the dining room doors to open.) But the virtuoso performance, for my money, is James Dickey's "The Firebombing." Written twenty years after the event, this 317-line poem takes you on a night solo mission, an "anti-morale" raid on Beppo, a small resort town in Japan. It's a wild ride and every detail is lovingly recalled. "The 'teardrop-shaped' 300-gallon drop-tanks / Filled with napalm and gasoline." "Combat booze by my side in a cratered canteen, / Bourbon frighteningly mixed / With GI pineapple juice."

The heart of the poem is Dickey's imaginative recreation of what probably happened when those silvery tear-drop-shaped tanks were released.

All leashes of dogs
Break under the first bomb, around those
In bed, or late in the public baths: around those
Who inch forward on their hands
Into medicinal waters.
Their heads come up with a roar
Of Chicago fire:
Come up with the carp pond showing
The bathhouse upside down,
Standing stiller to show it more
As I sail artistically over
The resort town followed by farms,
Singing and twisting
All the handles in heaven   kicking
The small cattle off their feet
In a red costly blast
Flinging jelly over the walls
As in a chemical war-
fare field demonstration.

How do you take responsibility for that kind of dam-
age? Jarrell absolved his 8th Air Force crew members of
the guilt that Dickey grabs for himself and revels in: "My
hat should crawl on my head / In streetcars, thinking of
it, / The fat on my body should pale." The other poets who
saw aerial combat (including me) show no such concerns.
William Stafford, a conscientious objector during the war,
takes notice of this in "Some Remarks When Richard Hugo
Came." Hugo was a bombardier in Europe who wrote
about the experience, and Stafford's poem begins:

Some war, I bomb their towns from five
miles high, the flower of smoke and fire
so far there is no sound. No cry
disturbs the calm through which we fly.

It concludes: "The bodies I had killed began to scream."

The face of war seen by those poets who served in the infantry is very different. It is close-up, in the mud, in front of you. The language tends to be grittier, maybe because the life was grittier. And the subject of rank often comes up: in the infantry the army caste system was more sharply defined than in the air force. Lincoln Kirstein, one of the best reporters of the war seen at eye level, discusses this in "Rank":

> Differences between rich and poor, king and queen,
> Cat and dog, hot and cold, day and night, now and then,
> Are less clearly distinct than all those between
> Officers and us: enlisted men.

He goes on to relate the story of a drunken, loutish officer who barges into an enlisted man's bar in France, stupidly shoots the patron's wife by mistake, and is brought before a military tribunal:

> The charge was not murder, mayhem, mischief
>   malicious,
> Yet something worse, and this they brought out time
>   and again:
> Clearly criminal and caddishly vicious
> Was his: Drinking With Enlisted Men.

Kirstein, who in France got to drive General Patton around in his Jeep, gives you Patton's talk, his character, his failings, his exploits in a four-page poem that is more satisfying than the movie.

The most down-and-dirty of the poets writing about the war on the ground is Alan Dugan, though he served as an airplane mechanic in the Pacific. His "Memorial Service for the Invasion Beach Where the Vacation in the Flesh Is

Over" is a horrific treatment of a subject that comes up several times in this volume: finding the bodies after the battle.

> I see that there it is on the beach. It is
> ahead of me and I walk toward it: its
> following vultures and contemptible dogs
> are with it, and I walk toward it. If,
> in the approach to it, I turn my back
> to it, then I walk backwards: I
> approach it as a limit. Even if I fall
> to hands and knees, I crawl to it.
> Backwards or forwards I approach it.

Even at their most quiet his poems are full of rage at the miseries of war:

> Sunday was calm and airy
> but artillery over the hill
> made us too nervous to like it.
> Some private tacked his tin
> mirror to a palm tree and shaved,
> using his helmet for a bowl
> that would not hold
> much water Monday night. . . .

That rage is also directed at authority ("the captain's football voice, / bully as acne and athlete's foot") and the state's power to send men "to an approved early death / under the national aegis." Studding Dugan's colloquial but formal diatribes are references to Homer and other Greeks. Fair enough: no poet took more pains to describe the many ways death is dealt out in war than Homer. The *Iliad* is a series of scenes of carnage linked by narrative.

An infantry poet who likewise makes use of the classics, Peter Viereck, in his "*'Vale'* from Carthage," describes how, as a soldier stationed in the ruins of Carthage in North Africa, he hears of his brother's death fighting near Rome. They had last met at Times Square. He borrows his *Vale* from an elegy Catullus wrote for *his* brother killed fighting for Rome, and ends his poem: "Roman, you'll see your Forum Square no more. / What's left but this to say of any war?"

The most traditional and perhaps most powerful of the infantry poets is Louis Simpson. His ballad-like descriptive poems move with ironic lightness over the carnage he witnessed:

> Arm and arm in the Dutch dyke
> Were piled both friend and foe
> With rifle, helmet, motor-bike:
> Step over as you go.

He uses the same tone to describe how he came to be wounded in battle: "I must lie down at once, there is / A hammer at my knee. / And call it death or cowardice, / Don't count again on me." The force of these seemingly simple poems comes from lucid narration, sharp, compressed detail, the use of ballad-like questions and answers, but also from an underlying sense (partly derived from the poem's clear references to the imagery of World War I) that his infantryman is archetypal and looms large against the sky.

Richard Wilbur and Anthony Hecht, who both served in the infantry in Europe, are sometimes criticized (wrongly, I think) as decorative formalists. Their war poems belie this. Particularly impressive, Wilbur's "Mined Country" not only tells you what the French countryside was like when land mines were laid—"Cows in mid-munch go splattered over the sky"—but explains how this subversion of the pastoral disinherits the child in us and alters completely our attitude toward the world. It is a poem that becomes much larger than its subject.

Anthony Hecht, in his Holocaust poem "Rites and Ceremonies," written twenty years after his return from Germany where as an infantryman he had seen the death camps, begins with a passage whose rhythm and language bring to mind the famous opening of Gerard Manley Hopkins' "The Wreck of the *Deutschland*." To quote Hecht's poem:

> Furnisher, hinger of heaven, who bound
>   the lovely Pleaides,
> entered the perfect treasuries of the snow,
>   established the round
> course of the world, birth, death and disease
>   and caused to grow
> veins, brains, bones in me, to breathe and sing
>   fashioned me air,

Hecht invokes "The Wreck of the *Deutschland*" presumably because Hopkins was a Jesuit priest and the Church at the time of the Holocaust did little more than deplore the slaughter (this is said explicitly in the poem). Hopkins was writing about the wreck of a ship, Hecht is writing about the spiritual death of a nation. It is a brilliant "literary" poem in which a very civilized poet describes unspeakable crimes.

Because poets appear in the anthology according to their date of birth, the first eleven to appear are civilians. In effect, their work forms a prelude to the volume. Though each of the civilian poets has his or her own take on the war, it may be that Conrad Aiken's line—"How can we patch our world up, now it's broken?"—speaks for all of them.

That these older poets—Jeffers, Tate, Winters—greet the war without enthusiasm is a reflection of the climate of opinion that preceded our entry into it. Most Americans were wary of getting involved in what they perceived to be a power struggle among Europeans. I remember as a child listening to Eddie Cantor, a popular comic of the time, end each of his Sunday-night broadcasts with a song that began, "The dogs of war are barking" and ended "Let them keep it over there." As a kid in public school and then as an adolescent reading journals on the political left like the tabloid *PM* and the magazine *Ken*, I was taught that wars were instigated by Big Money and fought for hidden commercial reasons. The exception was the Spanish Civil War: to defend the Republic was to fight for a just cause. Those who in the parlance of the time were called "fellow travelers," following Moscow's lead during the period of the Hitler-Stalin pact, adamantly argued against America's involvement; they reversed themselves when Germany invaded Russia in June 1941. For most of America, the climate changed with Pearl Harbor, but it did not change overnight.

Among these older poets is one who did participate vociferously in the politics of his time, but on the Fascist side: Ezra Pound. He is represented by lines from *The Pisan Cantos*, written during his imprisonment by the American army in Italy for treasonous broadcasts during the war. The lines are an indelible part of the landscape of that war, and so are included here.

Most of this book consists of work by writers who saw service during the war. Of the 62 poets included, 40 served in either the army, navy, air force, or merchant marine; and since those poets are allotted more pages than the others, about three-quarters of the book is theirs. The point was not to set up a caste system among the poets, but to present as many poems as possible that were written directly out of the experience of war, poems that contained the sights, sounds, and emotions of the war. Some were written during the war and some years later, but all convey the immediacy of the experience.

The civilian poets were chosen because they had significant things to say about the war, how it appeared to those at home, or because they wrote about important war-related issues not covered by the war poets themselves. Segregation, for instance. The American army during World War II was completely segregated in a system that was as rigid and bizarre as segregation in the American South. One example: I was a gunner in an all-white B-17 crew flying out of southern Italy. All the combat crewmen in my bomb group were white—officers and enlisted men alike. Yet frequently over our targets in Germany, we were covered by black pilots from an all-black P51 fighter group, also stationed in southern Italy, known as the Tuskegee Airmen (after the Alabama college where they had trained). We met only in the air. Poems by Witter Bynner, Woody Guthrie, and Gwendolyn Brooks address this subject. That said, it should be noted that this book does not seek to tell the story of the war; many crucial episodes are necessarily left out or touched on only briefly.

Readers will not find these poems antique. Not that much has changed stylistically since the time they were written. There are various identifiable influences at work: Auden, for one, whose traces I see in Karl Shapiro's "Scyros," for example. Some poets are affected by the populist rhetoric of the 1930s or by their political allegiances. George Oppen, who had been a member of the Communist Party, wrote no poetry while he was a member, a period that lasted for more than twenty years, because, as he said to me more than once, he did not want to be told what to write by the Party. But in the section of his poem "Of Being Numerous," one can see the political rhetoric he is jumping off from. In the work of Thomas McGrath, another Party member, one sees that rhetoric plainly.

There are Objectivists here, Imagists, followers of the Southern school of formal verse and dense rhetoric exemplified by two early poems of Robert Lowell, written when (to quote Lowell's later "Memories of West Street and Lepke") he was a "fire-breathing Catholic C.O." Comparing this body of poetry with the poetry of World War I, you can see how movies have altered the poet's vision. There are direct references to film, similes using film; there is Ben Belitt's long filmic poem about the infantry. Throughout, maybe as a way of distancing themselves from the perilous action or from their own actions, poets seem to be viewing a movie in which their lives are played out.

World War II marked the beginning of "The American Century," as Henry Luce called it in the title of a book published in 1941. Toward the end of the war, Walter Lippmann wrote: "What Rome was to the ancient world, what Great Britain has been to the modern world, America is to be to the world of tomorrow." Whatever the calendar shows, we seem, at this writing, to be strenuously caught in the drama of that American Century now. Never since World War II, not even in the Vietnam period, have so many individual American lives been affected by our national role. Because of this—quite aside from their own virtues—these poems of a war fought over fifty years ago continue to speak to the present moment.

Harvey Shapiro
2002

Defeat

On a train in Texas German prisoners eat
With white American soldiers, seat by seat,
While black American soldiers sit apart,
The white men eating meat, the black men heart.
Now, with that other war a century done,
Not the live North but the dead South has won,
Not yet a riven nation comes awake.
Whom are we fighting this time, for God's sake?
Mark well the token of the separate seat.
It is again ourselves whom we defeat.

EZRA POUND | 1885–1972

FROM Canto LXXXIII

Nor can who has passed a month in the death cells
    believe in capital punishment
No man who has passed a month in the death cells
    believes in cages for beasts

Δρυάς, your eyes are like the clouds over Taishan
    When some of the rain has fallen
    and half remains yet to fall

The roots go down to the river's edge
    and the hidden city moves upward
      white ivory under the bark

With clouds over Taishan-Chocorua
    when the blackberry ripens
and now the new moon faces Taishan
one must count by the dawn star
    Dryad, thy peace is like water
There is September sun on the pools

Plura diafana
    Heliads lift the mist from the young willows
there is no base seen under Taishan

    but the brightness of 'udor   ὕδωρ
the poplar tips float in brightness
only the stockade posts stand

H. D. | 1886–1961

R.A.F.

I

He said, I'm just out of hospital,
but I'm still flying.

I answered, *of course*,
angry, prescient, knowing

what fire lay behind his wide stare,
what fury of desire

impelled him,
pretending not to notice

his stammer
and that now, in his agony to express himself

his speech failed
altogether,

and his eyes seemed to gather
in their white-heat,

all the fires of the wind,
fire of sleet,

snow like white-fire pellets,
congealed radium, planets

3

like snow-flakes:
and I thought,

the sun
is only a round platform

for his feet
to rest upon.

II

So I knew his name,
the coming-one

from a far star,
I knew he would come again,

though I did not know
he would come so soon;

he stood by my desk
in my room

where I write this;
he did not wear

his blue tunic with the wings,
nor his cap with the crown;

his flying-helmet,
and his cumbersome trappings

were unfamiliar,
like a deep-sea diver.

III

I had said,
I want to thank you,

he had said,
for what?

I had said,
it is very difficult

to say what I want,
I mean—I want

personally to thank you
for what you have done;

he had said,
I did nothing,

it was the others;
I went on,

for a moment infected with his stammer
but persistent,

I will think of you
when they come over,

I mean—I understand—I know—
I was there the whole time

in the Battle
of Britain.

IV

He came again,
he did not speak;

I thought; he stands by my desk
in the dark,

he is emissary,
maybe he will speak later,

(does he still stammer?)
I remembered

how I had thought
this field, that meadow

is branded for eternity
(whatever becomes of our earth)

with the mark
of the new cross,

the flying shadow
of high wings,

moving
over the grass.

V

Fortunately, there was no time
for lesser intimacy

than this—
instantaneous flash,

recognition, premonition, vision;
fortunately, there was no time,

for the two-edged drawn-swords
of our two separate twin-beings

to dull; no danger of rust;
the Archangel's own fine blade

so neatly divided us,
in the beginning.

VI

He was huddled
in the opposite corner,

bare-headed, curiously slumped forward
as if he were about to fall over;

the compartment was crowded,
I was facing forward;

I said, put your feet up here
and I wedged myself tighter

and dozed off in the roar
and the train rumble.

VII

In the train jolt
our knees brushed

and he murmured, sorry:
he was there;

I knew in the half-daze,
in the drug and drift,

the hypnotic sway
of the train, that we were very near;

we could not have been nearer,
and my mind winged away;

our minds are winged,
though our feet are clay.

VIII

True, I had travelled the world over,
but I had found no beauty, no wonder

to equal the cliff-edge,
the line of a river

we had just passed,
no picture nor colour in glass

to equal the fervour
of sea-blue, emerald, violet,

the stone-walls, prehistoric circles
and dolmens

that I had just left
in Cornwall.

IX

True, we are cold, shivering,
and we ponder on many things,

waiting for the war to be over;
and I wonder,

has he come for me?
is this my particular winged messenger?

or was it tact,
a code of behaviour,

was it only a sort of politeness,
did he "drop in," as it were,

to explain
why he had not come sooner?

x

My thoughts in the train,
rushed forward, backward,

I was in the lush tall grass
by the burning beeches,

I followed the avenue, out of Tregonning,
across the fields to the other house,

Trenoweth,
where friends were staying;

there was the camellia-bush,
the stone-basin with the tiny lilies

and the pink snails; I remembered
the Scilly Islands off the coast,

and other islands,
the isles of Greece

whose stone thresholds (nor Karnak)
were older

than the sun-circles I had just left;
I thought of Stonehenge,

I thought,
we will be saved yet.

    XI

He could not know my thoughts,
but between us,

the shuttle sped,
passed back,

the invisible web,
bound us;

whatever we thought or said,
we were people who had crossed over,

we had already crashed,
we were already dead.

    XII

If I dare recall
his last swift grave smile,

I award myself
some inch of ribbon

for valour,
such as he wore,

for I am stricken
as never before,

by the thought
of ineptitude, sloth, evil

that prosper,
while such as he fall.

London,
17th September, 1941

ROBINSON JEFFERS | 1887–1962

Pearl Harbor

I

Here are the fireworks. The men who conspired and
　　labored
To embroil this republic in the wreck of Europe have
　　got their bargain,—
And a bushel more. As for me, what can I do but fly the
　　national flag from the top of the tower,—
America has neither race nor religion nor its own
　　language: nation or nothing.

　　　　Stare, little tower,
Confidently across the Pacific, the flag on your head. I
　　built you at the other war's end,
And the sick peace; I based you on living rock, granite
　　on granite; I said, "Look, you gray stones:
Civilization is sick: stand awhile and be quiet and drink
　　the sea-wind, you will survive
Civilization."

　　　　But now I am old, and Oh stones be
　　modest. Look, little tower:
This dust blowing is only the British Empire; these torn
　　leaves flying

Are only Europe; the wind is the plane-propellers; the
      smoke is Tokyo. The child with the butchered throat
Was too young to be named. Look no farther ahead.

    II

The war that we have carefully for years provoked
Catches us unprepared, amazed and indignant. Our
      warships are shot
Like sitting ducks and our planes like nest-birds, both
      our coasts ridiculously panicked,
And our leaders make orations. This is the people
That hopes to impose on the whole planetary world
An American peace.

            (Oh, we'll not lose our war: my money on
      amazed Gulliver
And his horse-pistols.)

          Meanwhile our prudent officers
Have cleared the coast-long ocean of ships and fishing-
      craft, the sky of planes, the windows of light: these
      clearings
Make a great beauty. Watch the wide sea; there is noth-
      ing human; its gulls have it. Watch the wide sky
All day clean of machines; only at dawn and dusk one
      military hawk passes
High on patrol. Walk at night in the black-out,
The firefly lights that used to line the long shore
Are all struck dumb; shut are the shops, mouse-dark the
      houses. Here the prehuman dignity of night
Stands, as it was before and will be again. Oh beautiful
Darkness and silence, the two eyes that see God; great
      staring eyes.

The Bloody Sire

It is not bad. Let them play.
Let the guns bark and the bombing-plane
Speak his prodigious blasphemies.
It is not bad, it is high time,
Stark violence is still the sire of all the world's values.

What but the wolf's tooth whittled so fine
The fleet limbs of the antelope?
What but fear winged the birds, and hunger
Jewelled with such eyes the great goshawk's head?
Violence has been the sire of all the world's values.

Who would remember Helen's face
Lacking the terrible halo of spears?
Who formed Christ but Herod and Caesar,
The cruel and bloody victories of Caesar?
Violence, the bloody sire of all the world's values.

Never weep, let them play,
Old violence is not too old to beget new values.

MARIANNE MOORE | 1887–1972

"Keeping Their World Large"

All too literally, their flesh and their spirit are our shield
New York Times, *June 7, 1944*

I should like to see that country's tiles, bedrooms,
stone patios
        and ancient wells: Rinaldo
Caramonica's the cobbler's, Frank Sblendorio's
        and Dominick Angelastro's country—
        the grocer's, the iceman's, the dancer's—the
beautiful Miss Damiano's; wisdom's

        and all angels' Italy, this Christmas Day
this Christmas year.
        A noiseless piano, an
innocent war, the heart that can act against itself. Here,
        each unlike and all alike, could
        so many—stumbling, falling, multiplied
till bodies lay as ground to walk on—

        "If Christ and the apostles died in vain,
I'll die in vain with them"
        against this way of victory.
That forest of white crosses!
        My eyes won't close to it.

All laid like animals for sacrifice—
like Isaac on the mount,
            were their own sacrifice.

        Marching to death, marching to life?
"Keeping their world large,"
            whose spirits and whose bodies
all too literally were our shield,
            are still our shield.

        They fought the enemy,
we fight fat living and self-pity.
        Shine, o shine,
            unfalsifying sun, on this sick scene.

Three Star Final

Wait here, and I'll be back, though the hours divide,
and the city streets, perplexed, perverse, delay
my hurrying footsteps, and the clocks deride
with grinning faces from the long wall of day:

wait here, beneath your narrow scrip of sky,
reading the headlines, while the snowflakes touch
on scarce-dried ink the news that thousands die,
die, and are not remembered overmuch:

yes, the unnumbered dead, whom none esteemed,
our other selves, too late or little loved;
now in the dust, proud eyes unknown, undreamed,
those who begged pity while we stood unmoved.

How can we patch our world up, now it's broken?
You, with your guilty heart, wait here and think,
while I strive back through lies and truths unspoken,
and, in the suburbs, the sunset snow turns pink:

you, in this dead-end street, which now we leave
for a more expansive, a more expensive, view;
snow falling, on a disastrous Christmas Eve,
and neon death at the end of the Avenue.

CHARLES REZNIKOFF | 1894–1976

FROM By the Well of Living and Seeing

During the Second World War, I was going home one
    night
along a street I seldom used. All the stores were closed
except one—a small fruit store.
An old Italian was inside to wait on customers.
As I was paying him I saw that he was sad.
"You are sad," I said. "What is troubling you?"
"Yes," he said, "I am sad." Then he added
in the same monotone, not looking at me:
"My son left for the front today and I'll never see him
    again."
"Don't say that!" I said. "Of course, you will!"
"No," he answered. "I'll never see him again."

Afterwards, when the war was over,
I found myself once more in that street
and again it was late at night, dark and lonely;
and again I saw the old man alone in the store.
I bought some apples and looked closely at him:
his thin wrinkled face was grim
but not particularly sad. "How about your son?" I said.
"Did he come back from the war?" "Yes," he answered.
"He was not wounded?" "No. He is all right."
"That's fine," I said. "Fine!"

He took the bag of apples from my hands and groping
    inside
took out one that had begun to rot
and put in a good one instead.
"He came back at Christmas," he added.
"How wonderful! That was wonderful!"
"Yes," he said gently, "it was wonderful."
He took the bag of apples from my hands again
and took out one of the smaller apples and put in a
    large one.

VLADIMIR NABOKOV | 1899–1977

When he was small, when he would fall,
on sand or carpet he would lie
quite flat and still until he knew
what he would do: get up or cry.

After the battle, flat and still
upon a hillside now he lies—
but there is nothing to decide,
for he can neither cry nor rise.

ALLEN TATE | 1899–1977

Ode to Our Young Pro-consuls of the Air

To St.-John Perse

Once more the country calls
From sleep, as from his doom,
    Each citizen to take
    His modest stake
Where the sky falls
With a Pacific boom.

Warm winds in even climes
Push southward angry bees
    As we, with tank and plane,
    Wrest land and main
From yellow mimes,
The puny Japanese.

Boys hide in lunging cubes
Crouching to explode,
    Beyond Atlantic skies,
    With cheerful cries
Their barking tubes
Upon the German toad.

Marvelling day by day
Upon the human kind
    What might I have done
    (A poet alone)
To balk or slay
These enemies of mind?

I sought by night to foal
Chimeras into men—
    Decadence of power
    That, at late hour,
Untimed the soul
To live the past again:

Toy sword, three-cornered hat
At York and Lexington—
    While *Bon-Homme* whipped at sea
    This enemy
Whose roar went flat
After George made him run;

Toy rifle, leather hat
Above the boyish beard—
    And in that Blue renown
    The Gray went down,
Down like a rat,
And even the rats cheered.

In a much later age
(Europe had been in flames)
    Proud Wilson yielded ground
    To franc and pound,

Made pilgrimage
In the wake of Henry James.

Where Lou Quatorze held *fête*
For sixty thousand men,
    France took the German sword
    But later, bored,
Opened the gate
To Hitler—at Compiègne.

In this bad time no part
The poet took, nor chance:
    He studied Swift and Donne,
    Ignored the Hun,
While with faint heart
Proust caused the fall of France.

Sad day at Oahu
When the Jap beetle hit!
    Our Proustian retort
    Was Kimmel and Short,
Old women in blue,
And then the beetle bit.

It was defeat, or near it!
Yet all that feeble time
    Brave Brooks and lithe MacLeish
    Had sworn to thresh
Our flagging spirit
With literature made Prime!

Cow Creek and bright Bear Wallow,
Nursing the blague that dulls
      Spirits grown Eliotic,
      Now patriotic
Are: we follow
The Irresponsibles!

Young men, Americans!
You go to win the world
      With zeal pro-consular
      For our whole star—
You partisans
Of liberty unfurled!

O animal excellence,
Take pterodactyl flight
      Fire-winged into the air
      And find your lair
With cunning sense
On some Arabian bight

Or sleep your dreamless sleep
(Reptilian bomber!) by
      The Mediterranean
      And like a man
Swear you to keep
Faith with imperial eye:

Take off, O gentle youth,
And coasting India
      Scale crusty Everest
      Whose mythic crest

Resists your truth;
And spying far away

Upon the Tibetan plain
A limping caravan,
    Dive, and exterminate
    The Lama, late
Survival of old pain.
Go kill the dying swan.

YVOR WINTERS | 1900–1968

To a Military Rifle

1942

The times come round again;
The private life is small;
And individual men
Are counted not at all.
Now life is general,
And the bewildered Muse,
Thinking what she has done,
Confronts the daily news.

Blunt emblem, you have won:
With carven stock unbroke,
With core of steel, with crash
Of mass, and fading smoke;
Your fire leaves little ash;
Your balance on the arm
Points whither you intend;
Your bolt is smooth with charm.
When other concepts end,
This concept, hard and pure,
Shapes every mind therefor.
The time is yours, be sure,
Old Hammerheel of War.

I cannot write your praise
When young men go to die;
Nor yet regret the ways
That ended with this hour.
The hour has come. And I,
Who alter nothing, pray
That men, surviving you,
May learn to do and say
The difficult and true,
True shape of death and power.

Moonlight Alert

Los Altos, California, June 1943

The sirens, rising, woke me; and the night
Lay cold and windless; and the moon was bright,
Moonlight from sky to earth, untaught, unclaimed,
An icy nightmare of the brute unnamed.
This was hallucination. Scarlet flower
And yellow fruit hung colorless. That hour
No scent lay on the air. The siren scream
Took on the fixity of shallow dream.
In the dread sweetness I could see the fall,
Like petals sifting from a quiet wall,
Of yellow soldiers through indifferent air,
Falling to die in solitude. With care
I held this vision, thinking of young men
Whom I had known and should not see again,
Fixed in reality, as I in thought.
And I stood waiting, and encountered naught.

Night of Battle

Europe: 1944
as regarded from a great distance

Impersonal the aim
Where giant movements tend;
Each man appears the same;
Friend vanishes from friend.

In the long path of lead
That changes place like light
No shape of hand or head
Means anything tonight.

Only the common will
For which explosion spoke;
And stiff on field and hill
The dark blood of the folk.

The Witness

Through a black and gold day, while the bright elm
leaves
Fluttered by my window, larger than yellow butterflies,
And the gilded grasshoppers rose from brilliant grass,

Shapes fluttered by, shapes beckoned me through spaces
between
Black stems of elms; their greaves, their shields were
gleaming;
Their anklets clinked of gold, their crowns were tiered
and shone.

Gods, and godlike men, they rose from the page,
The Greek lettering drifting round their feet—leaves
of elm
In autumn. And I was their stunned and crying witness.

Through the black and gold fire of October
Flanked by flames in the mind—for the first bombs
were fallen on Hellas—
I saw them, the golden of Homer, the bronze heroes of
Aeschylus.

With voices of trumpets they told of survival,
How the smoke of book-burnings had left no reek in
their hair,
Or stain on the gold, or dark in the heart.

Like the gentle telling of bells over water,
They pitied the races laboring with such fervor toward
doom;
And they touched my mouth. And I was their stunned
and crying witness.

RICHARD EBERHART | b. 1904

The Fury of Aerial Bombardment

You would think the fury of aerial bombardment
Would rouse God to relent; the infinite spaces
Are still silent. He looks on shock-pried faces.
History, even, does not know what is meant.

You would feel that after so many centuries
God would give man to repent; yet he can kill
As Cain could, but with multitudinous will,
No farther advanced than in his ancient furies.

Was man made stupid to see his own stupidity?
Is God by definition indifferent, beyond us all?
Is the eternal truth man's fighting soul
Wherein the Beast ravens in its own avidity?

Of Van Wettering I speak, and Averill,
Names on a list, whose faces I do not recall
But they are gone to early death, who late in school
Distinguished the belt feed lever from the belt holding
        pawl.

A Ceremony by the Sea

Unbelievable as an antique ritual,
With touch of Salamis and Marathon,
Through what visions of rebirth and death
At Atlantic's blue, hot, and sparkling edge—

War's head is up, war's bloody head,—
The thirtieth of May beats through America
With here the band, the boardwalk, and the speeches
Masking with blaze the parted beach crowds.

The traffic still restless, the loudspeaker proud,
Young couples in swimsuits strolling hand in hand
Beyond the crowd, self-interested, not attending.
But comes a hush like shimmer of summer over all,

With solemn tones the names are called, John Pettingill,
Roger Ashcroft, Timothy O'Shaughnessy, Patrick
O'Shaughnessy, Olaf Erickson, Alan Hieronymus,
William Henry Cabe, Neil Campbell, Victor
     Giampetruzzi. . . .

Long pause after each name, as mother or father,
Grandfather or grandmother, uncle, or brother
Awkwardly walks through the entangling sand
With sheaf or wreath of flowers to the flower-waggon,

Burgeoning with brightness beneath the bandstand.
The newly dead! The young, the dead far away,

In the strange young reality of their war deaths
Too young for this austere memorial.

The last name is called, the last flower is funded,
As people stand in the daze of the actual,
Then eight young men of the Army and Navy,
Almost naked, strong swimmers of the tides of life,

Their muscles blending in among the flowers,
Take up, four each, the flower-twined ropes.
Like a mad disturbance, hafts to the hilt of earth air,
Eighty Corsairs plummet out of the sky

From high inland down over the bandstand,
Four abreast, flash out over the sand
Over the ocean, and up easily and turn.
The deafening noise and closeness is a spell.

Then the flower waggon by the stalwart ones slowly
Through the crowd begins to go to the sea,
And as it draws, the ocean opens up its heart
To the heavy hearts of mourners by the sea's edge.

These, all kinds and conditions of men,
Thereafter follow across that bright, that transient course
As they would pay their tribute to the waves,
To the justice unaccountable of final things,

Followers of flowers; the gorgeous waggon-coffin
Drawing the blood out of the crowd, slow-passing it.
And lastly I saw an aged Italian couple
Too old to stumble through that catching sand,

The backs of their bodies bent like man himself,
Ancient as Marathon or as Salamis,
New and ancient as is America,
Diminish with laborious march toward the water.

From the platform funereal music played
In dirge that broke upon purged air
While now in mid distance, far by the shore, the new
    fated
Stood; then the powerful, the graceful youths

Like gods who would waft to far horizons
Drew the waggon in, which then a boat of flowers
They swam with, dim swan on the searoad.
A waiting gunboat fired a last salute.

FROM **Aesthetics After War: Instruments**

There are many intricate pieces of workmanship,
Precise instruments like the Mark 18 Sight,
With a floating reticle and a fixed reticle,
The fixed being a circle of light with a cross at the centre,
The floating being eight brilliant diamond points of
    light
In a broken circle which enlarges and contracts
Framing the enemy wingspan, increasing
As the enemy plane comes nearer, grows larger,
Decreasing as it flies away, grows smaller,

The whole floating reticle a dream of beauty,
But accurate to a split second of gunfire,
Its gyroscopic precision solving all problems
Of boresight, the pursuit curve,
Of wind drift, range, of bullet pattern
So that as semi-automaton all the young gunner
Has to do is to frame the enemy plane
In this brilliant circle of light and blaze away.
This is one of a bewildering array of imaginations.
Radar, as another expression of ingenious invention,
In its excessive, but already dated modernity,
Only gives man what bats have used for centuries,
Whose vibrations, beyond the reach of the human ear,
Strike obstacles which echo back to warn the bat
Who instantly evades each thing that would harm,
Although he seems to us to employ erratic flight.

Warfare spurs man to electrify himself with technics
But never can the human be contraverted
And as the Mark 18 Sight is only the fastest
Eye in the fastest brain, the perfectly anticipatory one,
And as radar is only an equal intelligence
To the ancient, instinctive knowledge of the bat,
So mankind in his abrasive rigors
Constructing the mazes of his complex aircraft
Often unwittingly makes them look like huge
Beetles or other insects, and I have seen
Hundreds of Corsairs parked in the evening glow
Their wings folded back ethereal as butterflies.
If a floating reticle in an electrical sight,
If a radar screen with its surrealistic eeriness,

If an airplane poised on the ground like a butterfly
Are beautiful, is their beauty incidental?
Is it man's limitation that his mechanical creations
Perforce cannot escape from his manhood?
And that try as he will, his works are human
And never stray far from the functions of the natural?
The mystery is whether the object
Mystifies man,
Or whether the mysteriousness within man
Transubstantiates the object;
Whether the world is finally mysterious,
Or if the Deity has put a mystery in man.

LOUIS ZUKOFSKY | 1904–1978

FROM **A Song for the Year's End**

I shall go back to my mother's grave after this war
Because there are those who'll still speak of loyalty
In the outskirts of Baltimore
Or wherever Jews are not the right sort of people,
And say to her one of the dead I speak to—
There are less Jews left in the world,
While they were killed
I did not see you in a dream to tell you,
And that I now have a wife and son.

Then I shall go and write of my country,
Have a job all my life
Seldom write with grace again, be part of the world,
See every man in forced labor,
Dawn only where suburbs are *restricted*
To people who take trains every morning,
Never the gentleness that can be,
The hope of the common man, the eyes that love
    leaves
Any shade, thought or thing that makes all man
    uncommon,

But always the depraved bark
Fight or work,

Dawn the red poster, the advertiser's cock crow,
Sunset a lack of wonder, the lone winged foot of
        Mercury in tie with a tire,
The fashion model
Her train stopped in the railroad cut
Looking up to a billboard of herself
As she goes home to her small son asleep,

So early and so late in the fortunes that followed me
        from my mother's grave
A lovely air follows her
And the dead President who is worth it:
'Dear death, like peace, I end not speaking,
The chitchat has died
And the last smile is unwilled
I am dead, I can't talk
To blossoms or spring in the world.'

STANLEY KUNITZ | b. 1905

Reflection by a Mailbox

When I stand in the center of that man's madness,
Deep in his trauma, as in the crater of a wound,
My ancestors step from my American bones.
There's mother in a woven shawl, and that,
No doubt, is father picking up his pack
For the return voyage through those dreadful years
Into the winter of the raging eye.

One generation past, two days by plane away,
My house is dispossessed, my friends dispersed,
My teeth and pride knocked in, my people game
For the hunters of man-skins in the warrens of Europe,
The impossible creatures of an hysteriac's dream
Advancing with hatchets sunk into their skulls
To rip the god out of the machine.

Are these the citizens of the new estate
To which the continental shelves aspire;
Or the powerful get of a dying age, corrupt
And passion-smeared, with fluid on their lips,
As if a soul had been given to petroleum?

How shall we uncreate that lawless energy?

Now I wait under the hemlock by the road
For the red-haired postman with the smiling hand
To bring me my passport to the war.
Familiarly his car shifts into gear
Around the curve; he coasts up to my drive; the day
Strikes noon; I think of Pavlov and his dogs
And the motto carved on the broad lintel of his brain:
"Sequence, consequence, and again consequence."

Careless Love

Who have been lonely once
Are comforted by their guns.
Affectionately they speak
To the dark beauty, whose cheek
Beside their own cheek glows.
They are calmed by such repose,
Such power held in hand;
Their young bones understand
The shudder in that frame.
Without nation, without name,
They give the load of love,
And it's returned, to prove
How much the husband heart
Can hold of it: for what
This nymphomaniac enjoys
Inexhaustibly is boys.

W. H. AUDEN | 1907-1973

September 1, 1939

I sit in one of the dives
On Fifty-Second Street
Uncertain and afraid
As the clever hopes expire
Of a low dishonest decade:
Waves of anger and fear
Circulate over the bright
And darkened lands of the earth,
Obsessing our private lives;
The unmentionable odour of death
Offends the September night.

Accurate scholarship can
Unearth the whole offence
From Luther until now
That has driven a culture mad,
Find what occurred at Linz,
What huge imago made
A psychopathic god:
I and the public know
What all schoolchildren learn,
Those to whom evil is done
Do evil in return.

Exiled Thucydides knew
All that a speech can say
About Democracy,
And what dictators do,
The elderly rubbish they talk
To an apathetic grave;
Analysed all in his book,
The enlightenment driven away,
The habit-forming pain,
Mismanagement and grief:
We must suffer them all again.

Into this neutral air
Where blind skyscrapers use
Their full height to proclaim
The strength of Collective Man,
Each language pours its vain
Competitive excuse:
But who can live for long
In an euphoric dream;
Out of the mirror they stare,
Imperialism's face
And the international wrong.

Faces along the bar
Cling to their average day:
The lights must never go out,
The music must always play,
All the conventions conspire
To make this fort assume
The furniture of home;

Lest we should see where we are,
Lost in a haunted wood,
Children afraid of the night
Who have never been happy or good.

The windiest militant trash
Important Persons shout
Is not so crude as our wish:
What mad Nijinsky wrote
About Diaghilev
Is true of the normal heart;
For the error bred in the bone
Of each woman and each man
Craves what it cannot have,
Not universal love
But to be loved alone.

From the conservative dark
Into the ethical life
The dense commuters come,
Repeating their morning vow;
"I *will* be true to the wife,
I'll concentrate more on my work,"
And helpless governors wake
To resume their compulsory game:
Who can release them now,
Who can reach the deaf,
Who can speak for the dumb?

All I have is a voice
To undo the folded lie,

The romantic lie in the brain
Of the sensual man-in-the-street
And the lie of Authority
Whose buildings grope the sky:
There is no such thing as the State
And no one exists alone;
Hunger allows no choice
To the citizen or the police;
We must love one another or die.

Defenceless under the night
Our world in stupour lies;
Yet, dotted everywhere,
Ironic points of light
Flash out wherever the Just
Exchange their messages:
May I, composed like them
Of Eros and of dust,
Beleaguered by the same
Negation and despair,
Show an affirming flame.

LINCOLN KIRSTEIN | 1907–1996

Snatch

Stained-glass panels shed their red as in a chapel to
endow
With rose reflection brass and bench, and bathe the bar
in ruddy glow.
Exhausted though still unrelieved, some GI's lounge
against the glass
To sip warm beer and drag dead butts and wait their
rationed piece of ass.

Near two full hours before high noon but in this whore-
home's smoky air
A stupefied narcotic pulse vibrates the muzzy atmosphere.
Too bright and early to make love; nervous fatigue
harasses haste.
We've just been dumped upon this town. We've fucking
little time to waste,

And vice versa. Here she comes, with nothing on but
rhinestone drawers,
To toss her tit and wink her twat and cense her scent of
musky pores.
Our soldier feels his courage stir, although he'd almost
just as soon
Hang around, bull-shit, drink and piss, and make it back
to chow by noon.

Yet sullen dreams of luxury unspent for starveling
    months to come
Inspire a blackmail base for lust to activate our beat-up
    chum.
Though he's no expert, still he can manage five-minute
    stiff routine
As skillfully as grease a jeep or service other mild
    machine.

Slips off his brakes; gives her the gas; dog tag and rosary
    entwine;
Moistures distilled from tenderness lubricate the kinky
    spine.
Well: up and at 'em. Now downstairs, the other joes
    have had theirs too;
They're waiting on him. Buzzy and smug, beer makes
    'em feel a shade less blue.

He slicks his cowlick in the glass; unchanged his mug
    her mirror shows.
His pecker limp, he pats her ass and blindly back to
    business goes.

Patton

Skirting a scrub-pine forest there's a scent of snow in air;
Scattered sentries in smart combat dress accord us their
    sharp stare;

My chaplain for the first time now allows as where we are:
>   At the core of this campaign.

Detroit's vast ingenuity subsumes our plans for doom,
Commandeers an auto-trailer to serve as a map-room;
Hermetic and impersonal, one may reasonably assume
>   This is Third Army's brain.

I spy a female nurse pass by, baiting a white bull-pup,
Official pet of General's and a humane cover-up
For isolated living or affection's leaky cup
>   At secret headquarters.

Nurse accepts my chaplain's solemn amateur salute;
He lets the pup lick and sniff his shiny combat boot,
Shoots her a semiprecious smile which all agree is cute—
>   Raps on that map-room door.

Should I from sloppy jeep jump out and to attention
>   snap?
Patton's informal entrance seems some sort of booby
>   trap,
But his easy stoic manner is devoid of any crap,
>   So I stick right in my car.

Measuring our morality or elegance in war,
I marked our nurse compose herself. Starch-white, she
>   primly wore
A gold-filled heart-shaped locket on her chest, and this
>   was for
>   Second, minute, hour.

Time's analysis is portable and only time can tell
What's in the works for all of us—nurse, chaplain, general.
Syllables in separate hour, minute, second, simply spell
       Military power.

Our brass cut short their conference, and Patton turns
       to me:
"Well, soldier, how about a cup of hot delicious tea?
Unless I am mistaken, Nurse may even add whisky."
       "Oh, thank you, sir," I said.

"Chaplain says you come from Boston. Then you know
       it is my home;
Now both of us are many miles from Bulfinch's golden
       dome.
By springtime it is where I hope the both of us may come
       Provided we ain't dead."

Nurse's watch ticked its temporal tune. Chaplain and I
       returned
To our base of operations whilst vict'ries blazed and
       burned.
Reckless Patton's vehicle one year later overturned:
       I see him as a saint.

Angels who flanked his final fling to martial glory's niche
Named Lucifer as honor guard, for that son of a bitch
My immortal captain's mortal, and also he touched pitch;
       His stars tarnished from taint.

In *Stars & Stripes* we read it when he slapped that
    soldier down
Cringing in a psycho-ward to play the coward clown,
Presuming to a state of shock (he'd smashed a stubborn
    town),
        But Patton blew his stack.

For me and my companions whom slap and shock stung
    too
Though minimal responsible find other factors true:
The pathos in enlisted men's not special to the few;
        It is the generals' lack.

Inspecting cots of amputees, unshaken obviously,
Approves the stitch above the wrist, the slice below the
    knee;
Hides in th' enlisted men's latrine so he can quietly
        Have one good hearty cry.

This soldier has to take a leak, finds someone sobbing
    there.
To my horror it's an officer; his stars make this quite
    clear.
I gasp: "Oh, sir; are you all right?" Patton grumbles:
    "Fair.
        Something's in my eye."

With vict'ry's brittle climax pity's never far away;
Patton feels only wounds should hurt which help him
    win the day.
But wounds have casual exits and it's often hard to say
        If blood flows in or out.

When endowed as a fine artist you can fling the paint
    around;
Or, called to seek salvation, you can make a solemn
    sound.
But crafty priestlike soldiers keep one premise as their
    ground:
        Loose fright ends up as rout.

Patton's a combat artist; hence his palette runs to red;
Makes superior generals anxious he's prone to lose his
    head,
Spoil pretty Rhenish landscapes with an April coat of
    lead:
        Our man may go too far.

The British and Canadians are ordered to push
    through;
Patton learns he's just their anchor with nothing much
    to do
But cultivate impatience, curse and sweat or curse and
    stew—
        Not his concept of war.

He vows: "Now you go fuck yourselves. I'm taking off
    from here."
He vanishes, nor hide nor hair. At SHAEF there is
    grave fear.
They bid him halt; he wires 'em straight: "I HAVE JUST
    TAKEN TRIER,
        SO SHALL I GIVE IT BACK?"

Military governor, Bavaria's shattered state,
He had a naïve notion which was not so all-fired great;
Hired him all former Nazis who'd nicely coöperate.
      For this he gets the sack.

And yet—it's not entirely fair. Since war is done and won,
Patton fears peace as idleness, peacetime as seldom fun;
Idleness is devil's business, and for the devil's son
      Good Nazis don't rank least.

This old pro was an innocent. Thank Christ for simple
      souls,
Pearl pistol-packin' poppa, prince of polo's thousand
      goals,
And I'm not fooling you, my friend: he starred three
      major rôles:
      Warrior, craftsman, priest.

We were rained right out of Nancy. Firm Metz we
      could not free.
Floods muddied fields; his bogged-down tanks less use
      than cavalry;
Came his orders: ALL PERSONNEL WILL PRAY THAT
      THESE UNSEA-
      SONABLE RAINS SHALL CEASE.

George Patton through proper channels forwards his
      request.
There comes logical reply to logistical behest;
Who am I to testify it's some joker's sorry jest?
      Rains cease. His tanks make peace.

Rank

Differences between rich and poor, king and queen,
Cat and dog, hot and cold, day and night, now and then,
Are less clearly distinct than all those between
Officers and us: enlisted men.

Not by brass may you guess nor their private latrine
Since distinctions obtain in any real well-run war;
It's when off duty, drunk, one acts nice or mean
In a sawdust-strewn bistro-type bar.

Ours was on a short street near the small market square;
Farmers dropped by for some beer or oftener to tease
The Gargantuan bartender Jean-Pierre
About his sweet wife, Marie-Louise.

GI's got the habit who liked French movies or books,
Tried to talk French or were happy to be left alone;
It was our kinda club; we played chess in nooks
With the farmers. We made it our own.

To this haven one night came an officer bold;
Crocked and ugly, he'd had it in five bars before.
A lurid luster glazed his eye which foretold
He'd better stay out of our shut door,

But did not. He barged in, slung his cap on the zinc:
"Dewbelle veesky," knowing well there was little but
beer.

Jean-Pierre showed the list of what one could drink:
"What sorta jerk joint you running here?"

Jean-Pierre had wine but no whisky to sell.
Wine loves the soul. Hard liquor hots up bloody fun,
And it's our rule noncommissioned personnel
Must keep by them their piece called a gun.

As well we are taught, enlisted soldiers may never
Ever surrender this piece—M1, carbine, or rifle—
With which no mere officer whomsoever
May freely or foolishly trifle.

A porcelain stove glowed in its niche, white and warm.
Jean-Pierre made jokes with us French-speaking boys.
Marie-Louise lay warm in bed far from harm;
Upstairs, snored through the ensuing noise.

This captain swilled beer with minimal grace. He
    began:
"Shit. What you-all are drinkin's not liquor. It's piss."
Two privates (first class) now consider some plan
To avoid what may result from this.

Captain Stearnes is an Old Army joe. Eighteen years
In the ranks, man and boy; bad luck, small promotion;
Without brains or cash, not the cream of careers.
Frustration makes plenty emotion.

"Now, Mac," Stearnes grins (Buster's name is not Mac;
    it is Jack),
"Toss me your gun an' I'll show you an old army trick;

At forty feet, with one hand, I'll crack that stove,
        smack."
"Let's not," drawls Jack back, scared of this prick.

"You young punk," Stearnes now storms, growing
        moody but mean,
"Do you dream I daren't pull my superior rank?"
His hand snatches Jack's light clean bright carbine.
What riddles the roof is no blank.

The rifle is loaded as combat zones ever require.
His arm kicks back without hurt to a porcelain stove.
Steel drilling plaster and plank, thin paths of fire
Plug Marie-Louise sleeping above.

Formal enquiry subsequent to this shootin'
Had truth and justice separately demanded.
Was Stearnes found guilty? You are darned tootin':
Fined, demoted. More: reprimanded.

The charge was not murder, mayhem, mischief
        malicious,
Yet something worse, and this they brought out time
        and again:
Clearly criminal and caddishly vicious
Was his: Drinking With Enlisted Men.

I'm serious. It's what the Judge Advocate said:
Strict maintenance of rank or our system is sunk.
Stearnes saluted. Jean-Pierre wept his dead.
Jack and I got see-double drunk.

P.O.E.

THIS IS IT and so: so long.
    We're soldiers now, all set to sail.
We may not sing one sad old song
    Herded within a dark dock-rail.

Self-pity pools its furtive tear;
    Expect the Worst, discount the Best.
Insurance as a form of fear
    Tickles the terror in each chest.

So: THIS IS IT—yet not the sheer
    Crude crisis we've been trained to take,
For many a female volunteer
    Doles out thin cocoa with thick cake.

They've parked their limousines the while;
    Their natty uniform is spick
And span, their hairdo and their smile
    Pronounces patriotic chic;

And THIS IS IT for these dames too.
    We strive to fake a grateful note
But goddam duffel bag and pack,
    Gas mask, rifle, helmet, coat

Too heavy are, so each sad sack
    Must flop and gripe: This is *some* shit.
Up On Your Feet, our orders crack.
    It's All Aboard for THIS IS IT.

GEORGE OPPEN | 1908-1984

Survival: Infantry

And the world changed.
There had been trees and people,
Sidewalks and roads

There were fish in the sea.

Where did all the rocks come from?
And the smell of explosives
Iron standing in mud
We crawled everywhere on the ground without seeing
    the earth again

We were ashamed of our half life and our misery: we
    saw that everything had died.

And the letters came. People who addressed us thru our
    lives
They left us gasping. And in tears
In the same mud in the terrible ground

FROM **Of Being Numerous**

I cannot even now
Altogether disengage myself
From those men

With whom I stood in emplacements, in mess tents,
In hospitals and sheds and hid in the gullies
Of blasted roads in a ruined country,

Among them many men
More capable than I—

Muykut and a sergeant
Named Healy,
That lieutenant also—

How forget that? How talk
Distantly of 'The People'

Who are that force
Within the walls
Of cities

Wherein their cars

Echo like history
Down walled avenues
In which one cannot speak.

CHARLES E. BUTLER | 1909–1981

Rifle Range: Louisiana

Sunlight streams from the cloudless southern sky;
Upon the warm and dusty ground we lie,
Rehearsing the gesture by which a man will die.

Do not pull the trigger: squeeze, instead,
Gradually, so that you will not know
The instant of persuasion and release:
(Nor will the soldier who receives the lead
Be quite aware of the instant he is dead
And perhaps at peace.)
Neither the slayer nor the slain
Will be quite aware:
They will share
The ignorance of the pain:
At least so we are told.

In the distance willows tremble in a wind;
The warm dust blows;
Death finds the paper target; neither the mind
Nor the finger knows.

The stillness bleeds with the sound of the bullet's curse,
The obscene cry,
And in the summer sunlight men rehearse
That men may die.

ROBERT FITZGERALD | 1910–1985

Pacific

"I am green under my cloud," the island said,
At dawn in a dim glass on the port side,
Foresail dovebreasted leaning to that bride,
Hesperidean, in her blossoming bed.

Target enlarging, gunned in the needling roar
Until drawn downward under ponderous blood,
We left her rocket-torn perimeter
As the pale brain labored for altitude.

Amphibians

I

The convoy under a continent of storm
Enters a gloom, a region floored by wind
With fleeces lifted from the dusk of ocean.

Air that was tender in the calms of summer
And touched the shining heads of waves and children
Veers like a runner on the serious sea.

Listen to the sound of the dark
Whistling and groaning: Meet her: the shrouded
  deckhouse
And deck descending sadly toward the blow:

A rumbling, then a burdened surge and frisking
Ramp of enormous water foaming away.

II

A trigger grip easily releasing a brilliant vapor,
A fanning plume: see how it licks up smoking
The starved and atrocious seafarer in its fire.

And down hell's terrace in a thicket rent
By the kicking rifle's shot a climber hit
In crablike sacklike slide and puppet's tumble

Dusts his flopping arm.
He must go blind out of the war and bleed
And die to breed again a busy darkness:

Rags of the sunny groin flies' hatching pit.
Be desiccate, O derelict in the sand.

Three American Women and a German Bayonet

Outweighing all, heavy out of the souvenir bundle
The German bayonet: grooved steel socketed in its
    worn wood handle,
Its detached and threatening silence.
Its gun-body lost, the great knife wrested to a personal
    particular violence—
Now bared shamelessly for what it is, here exposed on
    the American kitchen table and circled with the
    wreath
Of his three women, the hard tool of death.

And while Mary his mother says 'I do not like it. Put it
    down'
Mary the young sister, her eyes gleaming and round,
Giddily giggles as, the awkward toy in her left hand,
She makes impertinent pushes toward his wife who stands
Tolerant of child's play, waiting for her to be done.
His mother says 'I wish he had not got it. It is wicked-
    looking. I tell you: Put it down!'
His wife says 'All right, Mary: let me have it—it is mine.'
Saucily pouting, primly frowning
The sister clangs bayonet on table; walks out
And her mother follows.

Like a live thing in not-to-be-trusted stillness,
Like a kind of engine so foreign and self-possessed
As to chill her momently between worship and terror
It lies there waiting alone in the room with her,
Oddly familiar without ever losing strangeness.
Slowly she moves along it a tentative finger
As though to measure and remember its massive, potent
　　length:
Death-deep, tall as life,
For here prized from the enemy, wrenched away
　　captive, his dangerous escape and hers.
Mary his wife
Lifts it heavy and wonderful in her hands and with
　　triumphant tenderness.

BEN BELITT | b. 1911

The Spool

They splay at a bend of the road, rifles slung, the
shadows minimal, their hands tugging their slings by
the upper swivel to ease the routine of the march.
They have been moving since morning, and over each
has descended that singleness, mournful and
comatose, which is the mysterious gift of the march.
Their helmets shadow their eyes, their chinstraps
dangling. In the raddle of grasses their solitude
floats in a drift of identities, a common melancholy.

A captain enters the frame at the head of his
company. His face flashes. With his left hand he tilts
back his helmet, while with his right he draws the
length of an elbow across forehead and nose, his
stained armpits showing dark. A bracelet flashes
behind him. The column recedes, rifles close over the
canted belts, moving up, the packed backs vulnerable:
(Cut)
Late afternoon. In the half-light a handful of blazing
sticks, four infantrymen heating mess tins over an
eddy of smoke, a fifth on his hams, his eyes upcast
from the rim of his metal cup. Nearby a corporal
works a patch into the chamber of his rifle;
he repeats four syllables and smiles sleepily into

the camera. The camera moves to the bivouac area;
a group, their meat-cans close to their mouths,
spooning the compost, Chinese-fashion, and clowning
between mouthfuls. Very close. Their jaws,
lightly bearded, the necks in their jacket collars
strained in an easy horseplay, the Adam's apples
rapidly raised and released in the human exertion
of eating. In deep shadow, the light failing,
very close. A private tugs at his boot by the toe
and the round of the heel. Deliberately, he draws
the boot clear of his foot, sets it aside with deep
satisfaction, massages his instep over a maternal
thickness of socks. He bends toward the other foot,
camera-shy, a half smile breaking;

(Cut)

It is not yet possible to distinguish the forms
behind the camouflage netting. They move in the
central darkness of the gun, stacking shells and
bringing up powder charges. Only the bulk of the
howitzer is sure, the gun-barrel crossing the line
of the valley under the tented netting.
A village is burning in the valley. In the watery light,
smoke deepens over three hearthbeds of brightness.
A spire. A siding. A ladder of rooftops.
The gun fires. The picture trembles.

(Cut)

An iron darkening.
The hip of a tank darkens a frame,
foreshortened, the treads close to the lens,
a rushing of hammers, rings. The lens is cleared.
A cobbled street. A row of country-houses,

walled. A rosebush in the heavy light, blown
forward. Dust falls in the afterdraft,
a grain at a time. The camera is watchful.
A rifleman moves up the frame, his rifle at low port,
his shadow buffing the cobbles, crouched. He pauses
under the rosebush, his rifle hiked. A second figure
breaks through the frame, freezing between the
foreground and the far doorway. The man under
the rosetree sights carefully. The second man listens.
He raises his rifle, barrel backwards, and brings
the butt down heavily on the door-panels.
The rifle rebounds.
He measures a second blow, his teeth bared
slightly in a reflex of anxiety. His eye is large.
The butt-plate smashes over doorknob and lock,
the knocker flies upward once, the panel splinters
all at once. The man kicks the door open easily
with a booted foot. He listens, bent toward his
rifle-sights. He signals to the second man and enters
the doorway, stooped like a man entering a cave—

(Cut)

Brightness through trees. A damascene.
At the edge of a clearing, a parked jeep.
Two medical corpsmen lash litters to the jeep
engine a few hundred yards behind front lines.
The litter-poles enter the lens over the arch
of the engine. On the litter, a swathed head, a shock
of broken hair, motionless, a fall of blankets.
The stretcher-bearers vault lightly to their seats
and move off at a crawl.
Roadmarker: *Battalion Aid Station*. A corner of

charred wall, rubble, glass, timber. Legend: *Épicerie*.
The stretcher-bearers dismount.
The film is bad.
Presently a gloved hand in a surgeon's sheath,
holding a forceps. Briskly the hand moves over a
circlet of maimed flesh noosed in a bloody bandage.
A scalpel flashes between the living hand and the
human hurt, forcing the rind of the wound,
filling the frame. The camera submits, framing
the wound like a surgeon's retractor, its gaze
nerveless and saline. The gauzes blacken swiftly,
too heavy for the jaws of the forceps. . . .
The surgeon at full figure. A breeze finds the fold
of his tunic. In the distance the litter-bearers are
leaning for the litter-poles. His eyes hold the optical
center of the lens, unanswered. His mouth rejects
contemplation, not yet relaxed. His hands are void
in their glimmering cicatrix of rubber.

The City of Beggars

The wops came down to the port
When we docked
Dressed in the most fantastic rags,
Infantry caps on their heads
And feet tied in flour bags,
A garibaldian cape and throat scarved
With a dirty towel,
Half wild and half starved.
We threw them bread and cigarettes
Crowding over the starboard rail
To see what Italy was like.
They ducked their heads in an awful thanks,
Cramming the bread in a tin pail.
And we who had come on the foreign ship
Risking shark and submarine
Looked at the city the troops had won.
She lay in the Mediterranean sun
Under her moored balloons
With great holes knocked in her
As though with a wild hammer.
Fallen masonry and dust
Hanging balconies and stairs
Iron and iron rust
Abasso Il Duce on warehouse walls

And no glass anywheres.
Ruined and in ruins.
And American and Britisher
Who'd shelled her vias
And mined her waters
Hung on the pitted walls of their quarters
Their bulging aphrodites,
Rinsing their loneliness with cheap wine.
Morte del fascismo! Too late, too late.
The operatic dream and the reclaimed Caesar
Dredged from the swamp
Had climaxed in this:
Typhus and the walls down,
The gas escaping with a slow hiss.
And the adored jaw, the blared news,
To heat the mild Italian blood,
The second empire
From Tunis to the Nile
Had triumphed so:
The kids flopping in soldier shoes,
A cigarette picked out of the mud,
The bread depots and the water doles
In the tin cup,
The garibaldian cape shot full of bullet holes.

Italy, April 1944

HYAM PLUTZIK | 1911–1962

The Airman Who Flew Over
Shakespeare's England

A nation of hayricks spotting the green solace
    Of grass,
And thrones of thatch ruling a yellow kingdom
    Of barley.

In the green lands, the white nation of sheep.
    And the woodlands,
Red, the delicate tribes of roebuck, doe
    And fawn.

A senate of steeples guarding the slaty and gabled
    Shires,
While aloof the elder houses hold a secret
    Sceptre.

To the north, a wall touching two stone-grey reaches
    Of water;
A circle of stones; then to the south a chalk-white
    Stallion.

To the north, the wireless towers upon the cliff.
    Southward
The powerhouse, and monstrous constellations
    Of cities.

To the north, the pilgrims along the holy roads
    To Walsingham,
And southward, the road to Shottery, shining
    With daisies.

Over the castle of Warwick frightened birds
    Are fleeing,
And on the bridge, faces upturned to a roaring
    Falcon.

WILLIAM EVERSON | 1912–1994

The Raid

They came out of the sun undetected,
Who had lain in the thin ships
All night long on the cold ocean,
Watched Vega down, the Wain hover,
Drank in the weakening dawn their brew,
And sent the lumbering death-laden birds
Level along the decks.

They came out of the sun with their guns geared,
Saw the soft and easy shape of that island
Laid on the sea,
An unwakening woman,
Its deep hollows and its flowing folds
Veiled in the garlands of its morning mists.
Each of them held in his aching eyes the erotic image,
And then tipped down,
In the target's trance,
In the ageless instant of the long descent,
And saw sweet chaos blossom below,
And felt in that flower the years release.

The perfect achievement.
They went back toward the sun crazy with joy,
Like wild birds weaving,

Drunkenly stunting;
Passed out over edge of that injured island,
Sought the rendezvous on the open sea
Where the ships would be waiting.

None were there.
Neither smoke nor smudge;
Neither spar nor splice nor rolling raft.
Only the wide waiting waste,
That each of them saw with intenser sight
Than he ever had spared it,
Who circled that spot,
The spent gauge caught in its final flutter,
And straggled down on their wavering wings
From the vast sky,
From the endless spaces,
Down at last for the low hover,
And the short quick quench of the sea.

The Blinding of Isaac Woodard

(Tune: "The Great Duststorm")

My name is Isaac Woodard, my tale I'll tell you;
I'm sure it'll sound so terrible you might not think it true;
I joined up with the Army, they sent me overseas;
Through the battles of New Guinea and in the
    Philippines.

On the 13th day of February of 1946
They sent me to Atlanta and I got my discharge pin;
I caught the bus for Winsboro, going to meet my wife,
Then we were coming to New York City to visit my
    parents both.

About an hour out of Atlanta, the sun was going down,
We stopped the bus at a drugstore in a little country town;
I walked up to the driver and I looked him in the eye,
"I'd like to go to the washroom, if you think we got time."

The driver started cursing and then he hollered, "No!"
So, then I cussed right back at him, and really got him
    told.
He said, "If you will hurry, I guess I'll take the time!"
It was in a few short minutes we was rolling down
    the line.

We rolled for thirty minutes, I watched the shacks and
    trees,
I thought of my wife in Winsboro waiting there for me.
In Aiken, South Carolina, the driver he jumped out;
He came back with a policeman to take me off the bus.

"Listen, Mr. Policeman," I started to explain,
"I did not cause no trouble, and I did not raise no cain."
He hit me with his billy, he cursed me up and down,
"Shut up, you black bastard"; and he walked me down in
    town.

As we walked along the sidewalk, my right arm he did
    twist;
I knew he wanted me to fight back, but I never did
    resist;
"Have you your Army discharge?" I told him, yes, I had;
He pasted me with his loaded stick down across my head.

I grabbed his stick and we had a little run, and had a
    little wrastle;
When another cop run up with a gun and jumped into
    the battle;
"If you don't drop that sap, black boy, it's me that's
    dropping you."
So I figured to drop that loaded sap was the best thing I
    could do.

They beat me about the head and face and left a bloody
    trail
All down along the sidewalk to the iron door of the jail;

He knocked me down upon the ground and he poked
    me in the eyes;
When I woke up next morning, I found my eyes were
    blind.

They drug me to the courtroom, and I could not see the
    judge;
He fined me fifty dollars for raising all the fuss;
The doctor finally got there but it took him two whole
    days;
He handed me some drops and salve and told me to
    treat myself.

It's now you've heard my story, there's one thing
    I can't see,
How you could treat a human like they have treated me;
I thought I fought on the islands to get rid of their kind;
But I can see the fight lots plainer now that I am blind.

*I wrote this ballad on the 16th day of August in the year 1946, one block
from the wreckage of the Atlantic Ocean, on the beach at Coney
Island, New York.*

MAY SARTON | 1912–1995

Navigator

This lazy prince of tennis balls and lutes,
Marvelous redhead who could eat and have his cake,
Collector of hot jazz, Japanese prints, rare books,
The charming winner who takes all for the game's sake,
Is now disciplined, changed, and wrung into a man.
For war's sake, in six months, this can be done.

Now he is groomed and cared for like a fighting cock,
His blood enriched, his athlete's nerve refined
In crucibles of tension to be electric under shock,
His intellect composed for action and designed
To map a bomber's passage to Berlin by stars,
Precision's instrument that neither doubts nor fears.

This can be done in six months. Take a marvelous boy
And knead him into manhood for destruction's joy.
This can be done in six months, but we never tried
Until we needed the lute player's sweet lifeblood.
O the composed mind and the electric nerve
Were never trained like this to build, to love, to serve.

Look at him now and swear by every bomb he will
       release,
This shall be done. This shall be better done in peace!

JOHN FREDERICK NIMS | 1913–1999

Shot Down at Night

A boy I knew,
Arm gold as saddle-leather, lakeblue eyes,
Found in a foreign sky extravagant death.

Dreamy in school,
Parsed tragic Phaëthon and heard of war,
Arose surprised, gravely shook hands, and left us.

His name,
Once grey in convent writing, neat on themes,
Cut like erosion of fire the peaks of heaven.

The Arab saw
Strange flotsam fall: the baseball-sounding spring,
The summer roadster, pennoned with bright hair,

The dance at Hallowe'en,
The skater's kiss
At midnight on the carillons of ice.

Scyros

snuffle and sniff and handkerchief

The doctor punched my vein
The captain called me Cain
Upon my belly sat the sow of fear
With coins on either eye
The President came by
And whispered to the braid what none could hear

High over where the storm
Stood steadfast cruciform
The golden eagle sank in wounded wheels
White Negroes laughing still
Crept fiercely on Brazil
Turning the navies upward on their keels

Now one by one the trees
Stripped to their naked knees
To dance upon the heaps of shrunken dead
The roof of England fell
Great Paris tolled her bell
And China staunched her milk and wept for bread

No island singly lay
But lost its name that day

The Ainu dived across the plunging sands
    From dawn to dawn to dawn
    King George's birds came on
Strafing the tulips from his children's hands

    Thus in the classic sea
    Southeast from Thessaly
The dynamited mermen washed ashore
    And tritons dressed in steel
    Trolled heads with rod and reel
And dredged potatoes from the Aegean floor

    Hot is the sky and green
    Where Germans have been seen
The moon leaks metal on the Atlantic fields
    Pink boys in birthday shrouds
    Loop lightly through the clouds
Or coast the peaks of Finland on their shields

    That prophet year by year
    Lay still but could not hear
Where scholars tapped to find his new remains
    Gog and Magog ate pork
    In vertical New York
And war began next Wednesday on the Danes.

Troop Train

It stops the town we come through. Workers raise
Their oily arms in good salute and grin.
Kids scream as at a circus. Business men
Glance hopefully and go their measured way.
And women standing at their dumbstruck door
More slowly wave and seem to warn us back,
As if a tear blinding the course of war
Might once dissolve our iron in their sweet wish.

Fruit of the world, O clustered on ourselves
We hang as from a cornucopia
In total friendliness, with faces bunched
To spray the streets with catcalls and with leers.
A bottle smashes on the moving ties
And eyes fixed on a lady smiling pink
Stretch like a rubber-band and snap and sting
The mouth that wants the drink-of-water kiss.

And on through crummy continents and days,
Deliberate, grimy, slightly drunk we crawl,
The good-bad boys of circumstance and chance,
Whose bucket-helmets bang the empty wall
Where twist the murdered bodies of our packs
Next to the guns that only seem themselves.
And distance like a strap adjusted shrinks,
Tightens across the shoulder and holds firm.

Here is a deck of cards; out of this hand
Dealer, deal me my luck, a pair of bulls,
The right draw to a flush, the one-eyed jack.

Diamonds and hearts are red but spades are black,
And spades are spades and clubs are clovers—black.
But deal me winners, souvenirs of peace.
This stands to reason and arithmetic,
Luck also travels and not all come back.

Trains lead to ships and ships to death or trains,
And trains to death or trucks, and trucks to death,
Or trucks lead to the march, the march to death,
Or that survival which is all our hope;
And death leads back to trucks and trains and ships,
But life leads to the march, O flag! at last
The place of life found after trains and death—
Nightfall of nations brilliant after war.

Full Moon: New Guinea

These nights we fear the aspects of the moon,
Sleep lightly in the radiance falling clear
On palms and ferns and hills and us; for soon
The small burr of the bombers in our ear
Tickles our rest; we rise as from a nap
And take our helmets absently and meet,
Prepared for any spectacle or mishap,
At trenches fresh and narrow at our feet.

Look up, look up, and wait and breathe. These nights
We fear Orion and the Cross. The crowd
Of deadly insects caught in our long lights
Glitter and seek to burrow in a cloud
Soft-mined with high explosive. Breathe and wait,
The bombs are falling darkly for our fate.

Lord, I Have Seen Too Much

Lord, I have seen too much for one who sat
In quiet at his window's luminous eye
And puzzled over house and street and sky,
Safe only in the narrowest habitat;
Who studied peace as if the world were flat,
The edge of nature linear and dry,
But faltered at each brilliant entity
Drawn like a prize from some magician's hat.

Too suddenly this lightning is disclosed:
Lord, in a day the vacuum of Hell,
The mouth of blood, the ocean's ragged jaw,
More than embittered Adam ever saw
When driven from Eden to the East to dwell,
The lust of godhead hideously exposed!

Homecoming

Lost in the vastness of the void Pacific
My thousand days of exile, pain,
Bid me farewell. Gone is the Southern Cross
To her own sky, fallen a continent
Under the wave, dissolved the bitterest isles
In their salt element,
And here upon the deck the mist encloses
My smile that would light up all darkness
And ask forgiveness of the things that thrust
Shame and all death on millions and on me.

We bring no raw materials from the East
But green-skinned men in blue-lit holds
And lunatics impounded between-decks;
The mighty ghoul-ship that we ride exhales
The sickly-sweet stench of humiliation,
And even the majority, untouched by steel
Or psychoneurosis, stare with eyes in rut,
Their hands a rabble to snatch the riches
Of glittering shops and girls.

Because I am angry at this kindness which
Is both habitual and contradictory
To the life of armies, now I stand alone
And hate the swarms of khaki men that crawl
Like lice upon the wrinkled hide of earth,
Infesting ships as well. Not otherwise
Could I lean outward piercing fog to find
Our sacred bridge of exile and return.
My tears are psychological, not poems
To the United States; my smile is prayer.

Gnawing the thin slops of anxiety,
Escorted by the groundswell and by gulls,
In silence and with mystery we enter
The territorial waters. Not till then
Does that convulsive terrible joy, more sudden
And brilliant than the explosion of a ship,
Shatter the tensions of the heaven and sea
To crush a hundred thousand skulls
And liberate in that high burst of love
The imprisoned souls of soldiers and of me.

JOHN BERRYMAN | 1914-1972

The Moon and the Night and the Men

On the night of the Belgian surrender the moon rose
Late, a delayed moon, and a violent moon
For the English or the American beholder;
The French beholder. It was a cold night,
People put on their wraps, the troops were cold
No doubt, despite the calendar, no doubt
Numbers of refugees coughed, and the sight
Or sound of some killed others. A cold night.

On Outer Drive there was an accident:
A stupid well-intentioned man turned sharp
Right and abruptly he became an angel
Fingering an unfamiliar harp,
Or screamed in hell, or was nothing at all.
Do not imagine this is unimportant.
He was a part of the night, part of the land,
Part of the bitter and exhausted ground
Out of which memory grows.

                    Michael and I
Stared at each other over chess, and spoke
As little as possible, and drank and played.
The chessmen caught in the European eye,
Neither of us I think had a free look
Although the game was fair. The move one made

It was difficult at last to keep one's mind on.
'Hurt and unhappy' said the man in London.
We said to each other, The time is coming near
When none shall have books or music, none his dear,
And only a fool will speak aloud his mind.
History is approaching a speechless end,
As Henry Adams said. Adams was right.

All this occurred on the night when Leopold
Fulfilled the treachery four years before
Begun—or was he well-intentioned, more
Roadmaker to hell than king? At any rate,
The moon came up late and the night was cold,
Many men died—although we know the fate
Of none, nor of anyone, and the war
Goes on, and the moon in the breast of man is cold.

RANDALL JARRELL | 1914–1965

Eighth Air Force

If, in an odd angle of the hutment,
A puppy laps the water from a can
Of flowers, and the drunk sergeant shaving
Whistles *O Paradiso!*—shall I say that man
Is not as men have said: a wolf to man?

The other murderers troop in yawning;
Three of them play Pitch, one sleeps, and one
Lies counting missions, lies there sweating
Till even his heart beats: One; One; One.
O murderers! . . . Still, this is how it's done:

This is a war. . . . But since these play, before
    they die,
Like puppies with their puppy; since, a man,
I did as these have done, but did not die—
I will content the people as I can
And give up these to them: Behold the man!

I have suffered, in a dream, because of him,
Many things; for this last saviour, man,
I have lied as I lie now. But what is lying?
Men wash their hands, in blood, as best they can:
I find no fault in this just man.

The Death of the Ball Turret Gunner

From my mother's sleep I fell into the State,
And I hunched in its belly till my wet fur froze.
Six miles from earth, loosed from its dream of life,
I woke to black flak and the nightmare fighters.
When I died they washed me out of the turret with a hose.

Transient Barracks

(1944)

Summer. Sunset. Someone is playing
The ocarina in the latrine:
You Are My Sunshine. A man shaving
Sees—past the day-room, past the night K.P.'s
Bent over a G.I. can of beets
In the yard of the mess—the red and green
Lights of a runway full of '24's.
The first night flight goes over with a roar
And disappears, a star, among mountains.

The day-room radio, switched on next door,
Says, "The thing about you is, you're *real*."
The man sees his own face, black against lather,
In the steamed, starred mirror: it is real.
And the others—the boy in underwear

Hunting for something in his barracks-bags
With a money-belt around his middle—
The voice from the doorway: "Where's the C.Q.?"
"Who wants to know?" "He's gone to the movies."
"Tell him Red wants him to sign his clearance"—
These are. Are what? Are.
                              "Jesus Christ, what a field!"
A gunner without a pass keeps saying
To a gunner without a pass. The man
Puts down his razor, leans to the window,
And looks out into the pattern of the field,
Of light and of darkness. His throat tightens,
His lips stretch into a blinded smile.

O My Name It Is Sam Hall

Three prisoners—the biggest black—
    And their one guard stand
By the new bridge over the drainage ditch:
    They listen once more to the band

Whose marches crackle each day at this hour
    From the speakers of the post.
The planes drone over; the clouds of summer
    Blow by and are lost

In the air that they and the crews have conquered—
    But the prisoners still stand
Listening a little after the marches.
    Then they trudge through the sand

To the straggling grass, and the castor bushes,
    And the whitewashed rocks
That stand to them for an army and Order
    (Though their sticks and sacks

And burned slack faces and ambling walk—
    The guard's gleaming yawn—
Are as different as if the four were fighting
    A war of their own).

They graze a while for scraps; one is whistling.
    When the guard begins
Sam Hall in his slow mountain voice
    They all stop and grin.

A Camp in the Prussian Forest

I walk beside the prisoners to the road.
Load on puffed load,
Their corpses, stacked like sodden wood,
Lie barred or galled with blood

By the charred warehouse. No one comes today
In the old way
To knock the fillings from their teeth;
The dark, coned, common wreath

Is plaited for their grave—a kind of grief.
The living leaf
Clings to the planted profitable
Pine if it is able;

The boughs sigh, mile on green, calm, breathing mile,
From this dead file
The planners ruled for them. . . . One year
They sent a million here:

Here men were drunk like water, burnt like wood.
The fat of good
And evil, the breast's star of hope
Were rendered into soap.

I paint the star I sawed from yellow pine—
And plant the sign
In soil that does not yet refuse
Its usual Jews

Their first asylum. But the white, dwarfed star—
This dead white star—
Hides nothing, pays for nothing; smoke
Fouls it, a yellow joke,

The needles of the wreath are chalked with ash,
A filmy trash
Litters the black woods with the death
Of men; and one last breath

Curls from the monstrous chimney. . . . I laugh aloud
Again and again;
The star laughs from its rotting shroud
Of flesh. O star of men!

June 1940

*"Yet these elegies are to this generation in no sense consolatory.
They may be to the next. All a poet can do today is warn."*

*"The old Lie: Dulce et decorum est
Pro patria mori."*
            —WILFRED OWEN

It is summer, and treachery blurs with the sounds of
        midnight,
The lights blink off at the closing of a door,
And I am alone in a worn-out town in wartime,
Thinking of those who were trapped by hysteria once
        before.

Flaubert and Henry James and Owen,
Bourne with his crooked back, Rilke and Lawrence,
        Joyce—
Gun-shy, annoyers, sick of the kill, the watchers,
Suffered the same attack till it broke them or left its
        scars.

Now the heroes of March are the sorriest fools of April:
The beaters of drums, the flag-kissing men, whose eyes
Once saw the murder, are washing it clean, accusing:
"You are the cowards! All that we told you before was
        lies!"

It is summer again, the evening is warm and silent.
The windows are dark and the mountains are miles away.
And the men who were haters of war are mounting the
    platforms.
An idiot wind is blowing; the conscience dies.

The City as Hero

For those whose voices cry from ruins
For those who die in the dark alone
For those who walk the ruined streets

Here in your evening

The chimneys are empty of smoke
These squares of darkness are windows
The soundless wires stretch across the sky
Stillness of air
Under cold stars
And near the dry river
An old man without shadow walks alone

Upon pillows of darkness
Here is your evening

What words What answers now
What memories What ruined harbors?

WILLIAM STAFFORD | 1914–1997

At the Grave of My Brother: Bomber Pilot

Tantalized by wind, this flag that flies
to mark your grave discourages those nearby
graves, and all still marching this hillside chanting,
   "Heroes, thanks. Goodby."

If a visitor may quiz a marble sentiment,
was this tombstone quarried in that country
where you slew thousands likewise honored
   of the enemy?

Reluctant hero, drafted again each Fourth
of July, I'll bow and remember you. Who
shall we follow next? Who shall we kill
   next time?

Explaining the Big One

Remember that leader with the funny mustache?—
liked flags and marching?—gave loyalty
a bad name? Didn't drink, they say,
but liked music, and was jolly, sometimes.

And then the one with the big mustache
and the wrinkled uniform, always jovial

for the camera but eliminated malcontents
by the millions. He was our friend, I think.

Women? Oh yes, women. They danced
and sang for the soldiers or volunteered
their help. We loved them, except Tokyo
Rose—didn't we kill her, afterward?

Our own leaders?—the jaunty cigarette holder,
the one with the cigar. . . . Remember the pearl-
	handled
revolvers? And Ike, who played golf. It was us
against the bad guys, then. You should have been there.

Some Remarks When Richard Hugo Came

Some war, I bomb their towns from five
miles high, the flower of smoke and fire
so far there is no sound. No cry
disturbs the calm through which we fly.

Some day, a quiet day, I watch
a grassy field in wind, the waves
forever bounding past and gone.
Friends call: I cannot look away—

And my life had already happened:
Some saved-up feeling caught, held on,
and shook me. Long-legged grass raced out;
a film inside my head unwound.

The bodies I had killed began to scream.

Men

After a war come the memorials—
tanks, cutlasses, men with cigars.
If women are there they adore
and are saved, shielding their children.

For a long time people rehearse
just how it happened, and you have to learn
how important all that armament was—
and it really could happen again.

So the women and children can wait, whatever
their importance might have been, and they
come to stand around the memorials
and listen some more and be grateful, and smell the
    cigars.

Then, if your side has won, they explain
how the system works and if you just let it
go on it will prevail everywhere.
And they establish foundations and give
    some of the money back.

EDWARD R. WEISMILLER | b. 1915

To the Woman in Bond Street Station

Madam, you are right; the fight was a great pity.
Two soldiers against a third, an ally—perhaps
No worse could befall, as you feel, in this tense city.

Violence broke out so sharply: sudden fear
Fell on the watchers, who recoiled, and gasped,
And did not recall the girl who had disappeared.

Certainly the boy alone was very young.
It was brutal to smash at him so with the torch. But,
    madam,
Though what I mean, and would say, is not on my
    tongue,

It was late; all three are gone now, home to their places,
Their hatreds dimmed. And those who today are
    damned
Are not such furious boys with blood on their faces.

JOHN CIARDI | 1916–1986

Song

The bells of Sunday rang us down
And flowers were blowing across the town
Through faucets of the sun turned on.

For Mary's giggle and Martha's glance
The bankrolls flashed from pants to pants,
The Captain did a Highland dance.

Oh, there were troops in every door,
And liquor spilled on every floor,
And when the sun became a bore

We turned it off and hung a star,
For we were beautiful and far
And all the papers spoke of war.

And all night long from window sills
The Angels beckoned and the bills
Of visors turned and made their kills.

We burned like kisses on the night,
And talented and drunk and bright
We shed ourselves in colored light.

Because the train was at the gate,
And clocks were closing down the date,
And all seas were running late.

Elegy Just in Case

Here lie Ciardi's pearly bones
In their ripe organic mess.
Jungle blown, his chromosomes
Breed to a new address.

Was it bullets or a wind
Or a rip cord fouled on chance?
Artifacts the natives find
Decorate them when they dance.

Here lies the sgt.'s mortal wreck
Lily spiked and termite kissed,
Spiders pendant from his neck
And a beetle on his wrist.

Bring the tick and southern flies
Where the land crabs run unmourning
Through a night of jungle skies
To a climeless morning.

And bring the chalked eraser here
Fresh from rubbing out his name.
Burn the crew-board for a bier.
(Also Colonel what's-his-name.)

Let no dice be stored and still.
Let no poker deck be torn.

But pour the smuggled rye until
The barracks threshold is outworn.

File the papers, pack the clothes,
Send the coded word through air—
"We regret and no one knows
Where the sgt. goes from here."

"Missing as of inst. oblige,
Deepest sorrow and remain—"
Shall I grin at persiflage?
Could I have my skin again

Would I choose a business form
Stilted mute as a giraffe,
Or a pinstripe unicorn
On a cashier's epitaph?

Darling, darling, just in case
Rivets fail or engines burn,
I forget the time and place
But your flesh was sweet to learn.

Swift and single as a shark
I have seen you churn my sleep
Now if beetles hunt my dark
What will beetles find to keep?

Fractured meat and open bone—
Nothing single or surprised.
Fragments of a written stone
Undeciphered but surmised.

V-J Day

On the tallest day in time the dead came back.
Clouds met us in the pastures past a world.
By short wave the releases of a rack
Exploded on the interphone's new word.

Halfway past Iwo we jettisoned to sea
Our gift of bombs like tears and tears like bombs
To spring a frolic fountain daintily
Out of the blue metallic seas of doom.

No fire-shot cloud pursued us going home.
No cities cringed and wallowed in the flame.
Far out to sea a blank millennium
Changed us alive, and left us still the same.

Lightened, we banked like jays, antennae squawking.
The four wild metal halos of our props
Blurred into time. The interphone was talking
Abracadabra to the cumulus tops:

Dreamboat three-one to Yearsend—loud and clear,
Angels one-two, on course at one-six-nine.
Magellan to Balboa. Propwash to Century.
How do you read me? Bombay to Valentine.

Fading and out. And all the dead were homing.
(*Wisecrack to Halfmast. Doom to Memory.*)
On the tallest day in time we saw them coming,
Wheels jammed and flaming on a metal sea.

A Box Comes Home

I remember the United States of America
As a flag-draped box with Arthur in it
And six marines to bear it on their shoulders.

I wonder how someone once came to remember
The Empire of the East and the Empire of the West.
As an urn maybe delivered by chariot.

You could bring Germany back on a shield once
And France in a plume. England, I suppose,
Kept coming back a long time as a letter.

Once I saw Arthur dressed as the United States
Of America. Now I see the United States
Of America as Arthur in a flag-sealed domino.

And I would pray more good of Arthur
Than I can wholly believe. I would pray
An agreement with the United States of America

To equal Arthur's living as it equals his dying
At the red-taped grave in Woodmere
By the rain and oakleaves on the domino.

Elegy for a Cove Full of Bones

—Saipan
Dec. 16, '44

Tibia, tarsal, skull, and shin:
Bones come out where the guns go in.
Hermit crabs like fleas in armor
Crawl the coral-pock, a tremor
Moves the sea, and surf falls cold
On coves where glutton rats grow bold.
In the brine of sea and weather
Shredded flesh transfers to leather,
And the wind and sea invade
The rock-smudge that the flame throwers made.

Death is lastly a debris
Folding on the folding sea:
Blankets, boxes, belts, and bones,
And a jelly on the stones.
What the body taught the mind
Flies explore and do not find.
Here the certain stood to die
Passionately to prove a lie.
At the end a covenant's pall
Of stones made solid, palpable,
Moves the victory to the sea,
And the wind indifferently.

Hate is nothing, pity less.
Angers lead us to digress:
I shall murder if I can.
Spill the jellies of a man.
Or be luckless and be spilled
In the wreck of those killed.

Nothing modifies our end:
Nothing in the ruin will mend.
If I moralize, forgive:
Error is the day we live.
In the ammoniac coves of death
I am choked for living breath.
I am tired of thinking guns,
Knowing where the bullet runs.
I am dreaming of a kiss
And a flesh more whole than this.
I am pondering a root
To destroy the cove-rat's loot.
I am measuring a place
For the living's living grace.
I am running from the breath
Of the vaporing coves of death.
I have seen our failure in
Tibia, tarsal, skull, and shin.

Homecoming

After the cries of gulls and the fogbound island;
After the last accident, the last suicide, the last alert;
After we had broken the ties of separation;
After the ship, projection of desire,
              and the homeward passage;

When the country opened up like a child's picture
    book
(The hills were colored by our loneliness,
              lakes by the years of exile)
Until geography began to reassume its civilian status
And the slight smell of death was lost
              in the untroubled darkness;

Then we were troubled by our second coming:
The thing that takes our hand and leads us home—
Where we must clothe ourselves in the lives of
    strangers
Whose names we carry but can no longer know—
Is a new fear born between the doorstep and the door
Far from the night patrol, the terror, the long sweat.

And far from the dead boy who left so long ago.

Remembering That Island

Remembering that island lying in the rain
(Lost in the North Pacific, lost in time and the war)
With a terrible fatigue as of repeated dreams
Of running, climbing, fighting in the dark,
I feel the wind rising and the pitiless cold surf
Shaking the headlands of the black north.

And the ships come in again out of the fog—
As real as nightmare I hear the rattle of blocks
When the first boat comes down, the ghostly whisper
        of feet
At the barge pier—and wild with strain I wait
For the flags of my first war, the remembered faces,
And mine not among them to make the nightmare safe.

Then without words, with a heavy shuffling of gear,
The figures plod in the rain, in the seashore mud,
Speechless and tired; their faces, lined and hard,
I search for my comrades, and suddenly—there—there—
Harry, Charlie, and Bob, but their faces are worn, old,
And mine is among them. In a dream as real as war

I see the vast stinking Pacific suddenly awash
Once more with bodies, landings on all beaches,
The bodies of dead and living gone back to appointed
        places,

A ten year old resurrection,
And myself once more in the scourging wind, waiting,
    waiting
While the rich oratory and the lying famous corrupt
Senators mine our lives for another war.

PETER VIERECK | b. 1916

Kilroy

(for John H. Finley, Jr.)

1.

Also Ulysses once—that other war.

      (Is it because we find his scrawl

      Today on every privy door

      That we forget his ancient rôle?)

Also was there—he did it for the wages—

When a Cathay-drunk Genoese set sail.

Whenever "longen folk to goon on pilgrimages,"

Kilroy is there;

      he tells The Miller's Tale.

2.

At times he seems a paranoiac king

Who stamps his crest on walls and says, "My own!"

But in the end he fades like a lost tune,

Tossed here and there, whom all the breezes sing.

"Kilroy was here"; these words sound wanly gay,

      Haughty yet tired with long marching.

He is Orestes—guilty of what crime?—

      For whom the Furies still are searching;

      When they arrive, they find their prey

(Leaving his name to mock them) went away.
Sometimes he does not flee from them in time:
"Kilroy was—"
>*(with his blood a dying man*
>*Wrote half the phrase out in Bataan.)*

3.

Kilroy, beware. "HOME" is the final trap
That lurks for you in many a wily shape:
In pipe-and-slippers plus a Loyal Hound
>Or fooling around, just fooling around.
Kind to the old (their warm Penelope)
But fierce to boys,
>>thus "home" becomes that sea,
Horribly disguised, where you were always drowned,—
>(How could suburban Crete condone
The yarns you would have V-mailed from the sun?)—
And folksy fishes sip Icarian tea.
One stab of hopeless wings imprinted your
>*Exultant Kilroy-signature*
Upon sheer sky for all the world to stare:
>>*"I was there! I was there! I was there!"*

4.

God is like Kilroy; He, too, sees it all;
That's how He knows of every sparrow's fall;
That's why we prayed each time the tightropes cracked
On which our loveliest clowns contrived their act.
The G. I. Faustus who was
>>everywhere
Strolled home again. "What was it like outside?"

Asked Can't, with his good neighbors Ought and But
And pale Perhaps and grave-eyed Better Not;
For "Kilroy" means: the world is very wide.
            He was there, he was there, he was there!

And in the suburbs Can't sat down and cried.

"Vale" from Carthage

(for my brother, G.S.V. Jr., 1918–44, killed fighting the Nazis)

I, now at Carthage. He, shot dead at Rome.
Shipmates last May. "And what if one of us,"
I asked last May, in fun, in gentleness,
"Wears doom, like dungarees, and doesn't know?"
He laughed, *"Not see Times Square again?"* The foam,
Feathering across that deck a year ago,
Swept those five words—like seeds—beyond the seas
        Into his future. There they grew like trees;
            And as he passed them there next spring, they laid
            Upon his road of fire their sudden shade.
Though he had always scraped his mess-kit pure
And scrubbed redeemingly his barracks floor,
Though all his buttons glowed their ritual-hymn
Like cloudless moons to intercede for him,
No furlough fluttered from the sky. He will
Not see Times Square—he will not see—he will
Not see Times
                change; at Carthage (while my friend,
Living those words at Rome, screamed in the end)

I saw an ancient Roman's tomb and read
"*Vale*" in stone. Here two wars mix their dead:
   Roman, my shipmate's dream walks hand in hand
   With yours tonight ("New York again" and "Rome"),
   Like widowed sisters bearing water home
   On tired heads through hot Tunisian sand
   In good cool urns, and says, "I understand."
Roman, you'll see your Forum Square no more.
What's left but this to say of any war?

(Carthage, 1944)

Ripeness Is All

(pastorale for mine-layers)

Through nights of slanting rain
Marchers are planting pain;
    Gardeners in boots
Plant tender seeds of mines
Where the dimmed flashlight shines,
Nursing the wire-vines,
    Hiding the roots.

Boys in green raincoats scamper
Where grass will soon be damper
    When ripeness murders.
How fast the seeds grow high!
Blossoming, towards the sky
Pain's gaudy petals fly,
    White with red borders.

FROM **Beach Red**

Rejoice, O young man, in thy youth (Keep down, down.
Rest your body on your legs and on your arms
and for Jesus' sake don't let your pimply ass protrude.
Cradle your rifle in the bends of your two elbows
high enough so that no sand gets in the muzzle.
Now place your hands out in front of your head,
lift your belly and your chest slightly off the ground
and drag your carcass along by pulling with the wrists.
Crawl, dammit—not like a snake, but like a baby.)

And let thy heart cheer thee (So here you are,
of all the innumerable millions of men now and before,
at all the crowded intersections on the roadmap of eternity,
you and you only, placed by war's shifting of furniture
on this barren square foot of a condemned property
    island
to cover the spot where the rug's a little worn.
No, you don't have to fight. There's no compulsion
    whatever.
Nobody's talking themselves red, white and blue in the
    face
and only the sea is behind you if you turn.
It's just you and your firearm, the enemy and his,
and a perfectly democratic opportunity to use your own
    judgment.)

Walk in the ways of thine heart (Get up, now.
This is where you take the tags off your uniform.
Watch your step, and remember to shoot when
        anything moves
and move when anything shoots. Where are the little
        bastards?
Where are the orphans of heaven screaming,
        "American, you die!"
or "Iki, waki, konki, sookekki!"—spirit, harmony,
        stamina, total action!?
Nothing but trees wearing their hair parted in the middle
and sandalwood and frangipani and sago plants and sour
        mud
and camouflage suits mingling with foliage like visiting
        poor relations
and bullets sounding as though harpstrings were being
        impatiently tugged.)

And in the sight of thine eyes (Here are events
visibly projected in a changing kaleidoscope pattern of
        raw technicolor.
You see greenpainted faces and they are stifled with
        caution
as men advance in the mounting strain of sound effects.
There is quick, whirring action in a riot of noise
and darkness follows light, blinding the jerky blur of
        finality
as death turns over another page and resumes its
        commentary.
There is the crisp contour of destruction in startling
        sequence
and a corpse with its tongue stuck out at civilization

melts dimly away in a cross texture of coming
   attractions.
And the actors become stagestruck, stammer and forget
   their lines
because the script has suddenly demanded that they
   interpret reality.)

Yea, if a man live many years (Look. There's Mouse,
pushing a stern expression before him as he goes
   forward.
The calendar slapped him on the back and offered
   laughter
and pretty ankles and hot swing records and seats on
the 50-yard line and a coke at the corner drugstore . . .
And what of it, if no one will ever say
that this island battle was won on the playing fields
of Pembroke Junior College?) *Let him rejoice in them all.*

But let him remember the days of darkness. (The past
is beyond your influence, the present is something about
   which
you can do nothing, and the future is a mixture
of both. Let the guns argue about it among themselves.
Let the sand and the water debate as to who
shall extinguish your faltering flicker of life. And let time
break it into its component parts and pack them
   separately
and ship by express to the other side of tomorrow
and put the pieces together.) *For they shall be many.*

God will protect idiots, drunkards and Americans. It's
   His profession.

Negro Hero

to suggest Dorie Miller

I had to kick their law into their teeth in order to save
    them.
However I have heard that sometimes you have to deal
Devilishly with drowning men in order to swim them to
    shore.
Or they will haul themselves and you to the trash and
    the fish beneath.
(When I think of this, I do not worry about a few
Chipped teeth.)

It is good I gave glory, it is good I put gold on their name.
Or there would have been spikes in the afterward hands.
But let us speak only of my success and the pictures in
    the Caucasian dailies
As well as the Negro weeklies. For I am a gem.
(They are not concerned that it was hardly The Enemy
    my fight was against
But them.)

It was a tall time. And of course my blood was
Boiling about in my head and straining and howling and
    singing me on.
Of course I was rolled on wheels of my boy itch to get at
    the gun

Of course all the delicate rehearsal shots of my
        childhood massed in mirage before me.
Of course I was child
And my first swallow of the liquor of battle bleeding
        black air dying and demon noise
Made me wild.

It was kinder than that, though, and I showed like a
        banner my kindness.
I loved. And a man will guard when he loves.
Their white-gowned democracy was my fair lady.
With her knife lying cold, straight, in the softness of her
        sweet-flowing sleeve.
But for the sake of the dear smiling mouth and the
        stuttered promise I toyed with my life.
I threw back!—I would not remember
Entirely the knife.

Still—am I good enough to die for them, is my blood
        bright enough to be spilled,
Was my constant back-question—are they clear
On this? Or do I intrude even now?
Am I clean enough to kill for them, do they wish me to
        kill
For them or is my place while death licks his lips and
        strides to them
In the galley still?

(In a southern city a white man said
Indeed, I'd rather be dead;
Indeed, I'd rather be shot in the head

Or ridden to waste on the back of a flood
Than saved by the drop of a black man's blood.)

Naturally, the important thing is, I helped to save them,
    them and a part of their democracy.
Even if I had to kick their law into their teeth in order
    to do that for them.
And I am feeling well and settled in myself because I
    believe it was a good job,
Despite this possible horror: that they might prefer the
Preservation of their law in all its sick dignity and their
    knives
To the continuation of their creed
And their lives.

ROBERT LOWELL | 1917–1977

On the Eve of the Feast
of the Immaculate Conception: 1942

Mother of God, whose burly love
Turns swords to plowshares, come, improve
      On the big wars
And make this holiday with Mars
Your Feast Day, while Bellona's bluff
Courage or call it what you please
      Plays blindman's buff
      Through virtue's knees.

Freedom and Eisenhower have won
Significant laurels where the Hun
      And Roman kneel
To lick the dust from Mars' bootheel
Like foppish bloodhounds; yet you sleep
Out our distemper's evil day
      And hear no sheep
      Or hangdog bay!

Bring me tonight no axe to grind
On wheels of the Utopian mind:
      Six thousand years
Cain's blood has drummed into my ears,
Shall I wring plums from Plato's bush

When Burma's and Bizerte's dead
        Must puff and push
        Blood into bread?

Oh, if soldiers mind you well
They shall find you are their belle
        And belly too;
Christ's bread and beauty came by you,
Celestial Hoyden, when our Lord
Gave up the weary Ghost and died,
        You shook a sword
        From his torn side.

Over the seas and far away
They feast the fair and bloody day
        When mankind's Mother,
Jesus' Mother, like another
Nimrod danced on Satan's head.
The old Snake lopes to his shelled hole;
        Man eats the Dead
        From pole to pole.

The Bomber

Bomber climb out on the roof
Where your goggled pilots mock,
With positive disproof,
David's and Sibyl's bluff.
"Will God put back the clock

Or conjure an Angel Host
When the Freedoms police the world?"
O Bomber your wings are furled
And your choked engines coast.
The Master has had enough
Of your trial flights and your cops
And robbers and blindman's buff,
And Heaven's purring stops
When Christ gives up the Ghost.

The air is gassy and dry,
Bomber climbing the crest
Of the daredevil sky;
For this is the clinker day
When the burnt out bearings rest,
And we give up the Ghost.
At dawn like Phaeton
To the demolishing sun
You hurtled the hollow boast
Until you lost your way.
Now you dive for the global crust.
How can frail wings and clay
Beat down the biting dust
When Christ gives up the Ghost?

Bomber like a god
You nosed about the clouds
And warred on the wormy sod;
And your thunderbolts fast as light
Blitzed a wake of shrouds.
O godly Bomber, and most

A god when cascading tons
Baptized the infidel Huns
For the Holy Ghost,
Did you know the name of flight
When you blasted the bloody sweat
And made the noonday night:
When God and Satan met
And Christ gave up the Ghost?

Memories of West Street and Lepke

Only teaching on Tuesdays, book-worming
in pajamas fresh from the washer each morning,
I hog a whole house on Boston's
"hardly passionate Marlborough Street,"
where even the man
scavenging filth in the back alley trash cans,
has two children, a beach wagon, a helpmate,
and is a "young Republican."
I have a nine months' daughter,
young enough to be my granddaughter.
Like the sun she rises in her flame-flamingo
        infants' wear.

These are the tranquillized *Fifties*,
and I am forty. Ought I to regret my seedtime?
I was a fire-breathing Catholic C.O.,
and made my manic statement,
telling off the state and president, and then

sat waiting sentence in the bull pen
beside a Negro boy with curlicues
of marijuana in his hair.

Given a year,
I walked on the roof of the West Street Jail, a short
enclosure like my school soccer court,
and saw the Hudson River once a day
through sooty clothesline entanglements
and bleaching khaki tenements.
Strolling, I yammered metaphysics with Abramowitz,
a jaundice-yellow ("it's really tan")
and fly-weight pacifist,
so vegetarian,
he wore rope shoes and preferred fallen fruit.
He tried to convert Bioff and Brown,
the Hollywood pimps, to his diet.
Hairy, muscular, suburban,
wearing chocolate double-breasted suits,
they blew their tops and beat him black and blue.

I was so out of things, I'd never heard
of the Jehovah's Witnesses.
"Are you a C.O.?" I asked a fellow jailbird.
"No," he answered, "I'm a J.W."
He taught me the "hospital tuck,"
and pointed out the T shirted back
of *Murder Incorporated's* Czar Lepke,
there piling towels on a rack,
or dawdling off to his little segregated cell full
of things forbidden the common man:

a portable radio, a dresser, two toy American
flags tied together with a ribbon of Easter palm.
Flabby, bald, lobotomized,
he drifted in a sheepish calm,
where no agonizing reappraisal
jarred his concentration on the electric chair—
hanging like an oasis in his air
of lost connections. . . .

Soldiers in Death

So might you speak the world as who should know
it as a tragic and desired place
who saw its awful darkness face to face
yet grieved to feel its fluid substance go
between two hands not made to stay the flow;
who held, with the fairer world, in one embrace
these horrors that desire could ill erase
but felt the aimless void begin to grow.
Pity for your poor bodies, then, that died
their lovers' deaths and carrion lie, unfired
by love now, shameful and dumb in death's disarray,
that saw the dark by which your love was tried
and felt how carelessly the world expired
as a head might turn and look again away.

Memorial

If we do not lift quickly the dead bodies from the beaches
the tide begins to put them down like a disappointment
carried beneath the clothing, or hidden
in the intricate folded greyness of the brain.

Now we can know again, even more plainly,
how quickly the world changes.
The land and life too are interrupted
by the indomitable fantasy of extreme violence
and the awful terror.
The body, eager with its wants and its rich few years
is dead now on the beaches.

The war came as a water rising, leaving us homeless.
The easy company of the dispossessed was a grave joy.

On the crest of waters we invaded the distance.
Recession will find our shells far: high up in mountains.
It will be explained how they came there.
It will not be understood.

Epithalamium in Olive Drab

O orange were her underclothes,
   her nails were hothouse pink,
when Rosalind, in jungle rose,
   was wed in a roller rink.

        The bells ring true: True-blue True-blue.
        She was cheery; he was chipper.
        They did not fly to Ho - no - lu - lu
        in the cabin of a clipper.

With the frontal lobe of Jackie Cooper
   and the soul of General Grant,
Paul is now a paratrooper
   and Roz rivets in a plant.

        The bells ring true: True-blue True-blue.
        She was cheery; he was chipper.
        They did not fly to Ho - no - lu - lu
        in the cabin of a clipper.

They lie elate from six to eight
   at the Mars Moontide Motel.
Of the union I celebrate
   more I may not tell.

The bells ring true: True-blue True-blue.
She was cheery; he was chipper.
They did not fly to Ho - no - lu - lu
in the cabin of a clipper.

Pidgin Pinch

Joe, you Big Shot! You Big Man!
You Government Issue! You Marshall Plan!

Joe, you got plenty Spearmint Gum?
I change you Money, you gimme Some!

Joe, you want Shoe-Shine, Cheap Souvenir?
My Sister overhaul you Landing Gear?

Joe, you Queer Kid? Fix-you Me?
Dig-Dig? Buzz-Buzz? Reefer? Tea?

Joe, I find you Belly Dance,
Trip Around the World—Fifty Cents!

Joe, you got Cigarette? Joe, you got Match?
Joe, you got Candy? You Sum-Bitch,

You think I Crazy? I waste my Time?
I give you *Trouble?* Gimme a *Dime!*

Columbus Circle Swing

Old Mr. Christopher sailed an egg
to prove that it was round
while the man at the keg with the wooden leg
stood his ground.

Brothers Wright, perfecting flight,
let the rabbit out of the hat:
Now overhead the quadruped
disputes his habitat.

O where shall we go when it rains all the day,
and what shall we do when it's over:
will the day be as bright when it dawns at Calais
as it was after dark at Dover?

Bombers roar off overhead,
turn down your shaded lamps.
The cities burn, a Christmas red,
smoke rises from the camps.

The world's an egg, ah, through and through.
It was decided for us.
You can always change a line or two;
you cannot change the chorus.

O where shall we go when it rains all the day,
and what shall we do when it's over:
will the day be as bright when it dawns at Calais
as it was after dark at Dover?

ROBERT DUNCAN | 1919–1988

A Spring Memorandum: Fort Knox

The beginning of this year in spring is twisted,
closes in my mind with a perspective, clear
and precise as a medieval fortress, a map of walls and
    towers,
painted tents and geometries of distance. Here
        the tree
that from my heart sprang quick and green
dies at the throat. And as I turn
from these disorderd leaves toward the immediate
    scene,
        the dust
shifts, and the landscape burns the root
in its unyielding light. The guns
are new devices in the mind for absolutes, excite a
    curious art.
We lie uneasy on our bellies in the blaze. The eye
tires and the target—lung or chest,
        bursts,
shivers on the level edge of the front sight. And death
we see there painted as precisely as a medieval rose.
        The target
man has unreal clarity.

     *

We are strangely
innocent killers. Gonzales,
Daniel Garcia and I talk idly, lying on our bunks
before mess-call. We say that in September
there will be fiestas and dances in the bordertowns.
We do not talk of killing. We recall
how Gonzales playd the saxophone
at summer weddings in Laredo, and we were elegant
in white suede shoes. The war has not come. We say
the war will never come. We will be free. We speak
of Mexico and cities in the mountains, white
receding refuge in the mind; or at night
we hear from some other barracks a Texas guitar.

                    *

There is a reasonless
stillness still in us. The cells and the bodies
that hunger for freedom are restless but lie
like rocks in silence and resist the scene.
And the scene is unmoved. We are weary with marching.
Slow and deliberate, the last shelter lifts
          from the killing
and we stand at attention in the mechanized day.

The eye and the hand which trembled
when it first took the pistol grow steady
and directed to murder. In his two dimensions
the flat man is easily shot.

He might have been loved.
It would have been harder. We conceive
a small triangle with bullets
over his heart.

I am not native here. I am a fox
caught, baited and clampd. I will claw my way free
from the flesh, spring the lock at the wrist,
leap out there, leap away, power-dive to the darkness,
if the flesh is this nature.
I am not of this kind.

Or, because love remains, must there be life
putting out branches to cover its wound?
Why do I wait when they take from me hope
and burn out the wonder, for what country, what
Always, our dream of tomorrow, to be there
more real than this country? Consider in quiet
the leaves of light that appear, even here,
in this wilderness, tormented by God.

Enormous Worm, turning upon Himself in His cyst,
disturbing the night with His love, who
has seen Him? I found at the roots of a tree
where Randlett and I were lying in the late afternoon
an Imago, like dried paper, that we
as children called Child-of-the-Earth. Where
has He gone, I askt. Slipt from our bodies
as this insect slipt from his skin? We are vacated,
left in discard with a hunger no universe of love
can feed nor Calendar of Days fulfill. And yet,
each day the substance rises in the hornhide tree of self,
twists and reaches and seeks to flower in the light.

Navy Field

Limped out of the hot sky a hurt plane,
Held off, held off, whirring pretty pigeon,
Hit then and scuttled to a crooked stop.
The stranger pilot who emerged—this was the seashore,
War came suddenly here—talked to the still mechanics
Who nodded gravely. Flak had done it, he said,
From an enemy ship attacked.

        They wheeled it with love
Into the dark hangar's mouth and tended it.
Coffee and cake for the pilot then who sat alone
In the restaurant, reading the numbered sheets
That tell about weather.

        After, toward dusk,
Mended the stranger plane went back to the sky.
His curly-headed picture, and mother's and medal's
    pictures
Were all we knew of him after he rose again,
Those few electric jewels against the moth and
    whining sky.

Love Letter from an Impossible Land

Combed by the cold seas, Bering and Pacific,
These are the exile islands of the mind.
All the charts and history you can muster
Will not make them real as the fog is real
Or crystal as a certain hour is clear
If you can wait.
                    Write to me often, darling.

Thrown up hurriedly for a late-crossing people,
These are unsettled mountains where I walk,
They dance at the center still and spout new ash;
The teeming salmon remember in their courses
When they were not, and the winds run into the hills
By an old habit.

Now I am convinced there is nothing to fear,
Now on these islands you are all I want;
They shake and change and finally enchant;
But I have wished you a bawdy darling and here
Often, I, rootless and needing a quick home.

Here I have seen such singular strange visions,
So moving strong in beauty
You would not believe them, no
Not if your very lover told you so
At night remembering, stirred in my sleep at night.

One was, in the orange time of morning,
The smoking peak Shishaldin in a glory;
(Eastward I saw, oh, I remember eastward
Pavlof, the black volcano, throwing flame
At night, to seaward, when beacons were forbidden.)
Empedocles' element, neither earth nor fire;
And when I put a wing across the cone
(Snowy, and striking deeply at the memory),
It drew me, too, driven and weary
What with the war, and those foolish citizens my
     thoughts.

Another, the humorless mounds, the kitchen middens
Built in the painful winds that blow forever.
Watch the slow procession laying them down
(An almond-eyed people, parent to Incas and Indians)
Shell upon shell, bone upon bone, until
See they have builded there a little hill!
A thousand years, seated by this cold harbor, eating
     fish,
In what was to prove only a delaying action.

You are one for the day I landed there in sunshine,
Porcelain little village with your white Russian church,
Your far-eyed children and hollow-barking malemutes
That romp on the beach, cluttered with boats and
     flowers.
When was June gentleness set in so alien a land,
In a calendar with so few sunny saints?

A moon miracle are the milky hills at night
With streamers of snow dancing in the moon at the
     summits,
An ageless dance with the peculiar rhythm of zero,
And the wind creaking like a green floe.

And now I write you from such another vision.

As the haunted men who wrestle a weariness
Or women who languish from no sickness known
In books a century back, am I alone
In the sheer time of hilltop happiness.
Deft on the harbor I have put behind
The lovely gray vessels for their battles wait.
Twenty-four blue sailors anticipate
Orders of drill that drift up on the wind.
And stiff on the apron are the pretty planes
That waddle to the water and drum away,
Leaving me stammerer, inept to say
Why in their simple duty there is pain.

You will see in this passage I am wanting you.

Providence occurs to me;
I will salvage these parts of a loud land
For symbols of war its simple wraths and duties,
Against when, like the hut-two-three-four sailors
Disbanded into chaos by Fall-out,
I shall resume my several tedious parts,
In an old land with people reaching backward like many
     curtains,

Possessing a mystery beyond the mist of mountains
Ornate beyond the ritual of snow.

The moth sky of evening and the moth sea
Linger into night and coupling sleep.
Sleep for us here is a leaping down safely in silk
From the flaming bull's-eye plane of day,
Stricken ship that twists and thirsts for the metal sea.
We lie in khaki rows, no two alike,
Needing to be called by name
And saying women's names.

Now the moth descends, but when the dove?
God keep us whole and true, my distant love.

Simile

As when a heavy bomber in the cloud
Having made some minutes good an unknown track;
Although the dead-reckoner triangulates
Departure and the stations he can fix,
Counting the thinness of the chilly air,
The winds aloft, the readings of the clocks;
And the radarman sees the green snakes dance
Continually before him in attest
That the hostile sought terrain runs on below;
And although the phantom shapes of friendly planes
Flit on the screen and sometimes through the cloud
Where the pilot squints against the forward glass,

Seeing reflected phosphorescent dials
And his own anxious face in all command;
And each man thinks of some unlikely love,
Hitherto his; and issues drop away
Like jettisoned bombs, and all is personal fog;
Then, hope aside and hunger all at large
For certainty what war is, foe is, where America;
Then, the four engines droning like a sorrow,
Clear, sudden miracle: cloud breaks,
Tatter of cloud passes, there ahead,
Beside, above, friends in the desperate sky;
And below burns like all fire the target town,
A delicate red chart of squares, abstract
And jewelled, from which rise lazy tracers,
And the searchlights through smoke tumble up
To a lovely apex on some undone friend;
As in this fierce discovery is something found
More than release from waiting or of bombs,
Greater than all the Germanies of hate,
Some penetration of the overcast
We make through, hour upon uncounted hour,
All this life, fuel low, instruments all tumbled,
And uncrewed.

ANN DARR | b. 1920

Flight as a Way of Life

I used to tow targets
out of Las Vegas.
Canaries sang in their cages
in the gilded gaming rooms
not cheep, cheep, cheep but
    dear, dear
and early in the morning
when the sun struck gold into
    Boulder Lake,
there was their great golden
    egg.

A Fable of the War

The full moon is partly hidden by cloud,
The snow that fell when we came off the boat
Has stopped by now, and it is turning colder.
I pace the platform under the blue lights,
Under a frame of glass and emptiness
In a station whose name I do not know.

Suddenly, passing the known and unknown
Bowed faces of my company, the sad
And potent outfit of the armed, I see
That we are dead. By stormless Acheron
We stand easy, and the occasional moon
Strikes terribly from steel and bone alike.

Our flesh, I see, was too corruptible
For the huge work of death. Only the blind
Crater of the eye can suffer well
The midnight cold of stations in no place,
And hold the tears of pity frozen that
They will implacably reflect on war.

But I have read that God let Solomon
Stand upright, although dead, until the temple
Should be raised up, that demons forced to the work

Might not revolt before the thing was done.
And the king stood, until a little worm
Had eaten through the stick he leaned upon.

So, gentlemen—by greatcoat, cartridge belt
And helmet held together for the time—
In honorably enduring here we seek
The second death. Until the worm shall bite
To betray us, lean each man on his gun
That the great work not falter but go on.

A Memory of the War

Most what I know of war is what I learned
When mine was over and they shipped me home.
I'd been a chauffeur with the RAF
And didn't know the first damn thing about
The American way of doing anything
Till they told me I was Officer of the Day
(at midnight, yet) and gave me a whopping great
Blue automatic and sat me on D Deck
At the top of a ladder leading to a hold
Where a couple hundred enlisted men were sleeping,
And said I was to sit there till relieved.
"But what's this for?" I said about the gun,
And was answered: "If this ship shows any sign
Of going down, you shoot down the first son-
ofabitch sticks his head up through this hatch."
So that is what I did, and how I learned
About the War: I sat there till relieved.

Night Operations, Coastal Command RAF

Remembering that war, I'd near believe
We didn't need the enemy, with whom
Our dark encounters were confused and few
And quickly done, so many of our lot
Did for themselves in folly and misfortune.

Some hit our own barrage balloons, and some
Tripped over power lines, coming in low;
Some swung on takeoff, others overshot,
And two or three forgot to lower the wheels.
There were those that flew the bearing for the course
And flew away forever; and the happy few
That homed on Venus sinking beyond the sea
In fading certitude. For all the skill,
For all the time of training, you might take
The hundred steps in darkness, not the next.

The War in the Air

For a saving grace, we didn't see our dead,
Who rarely bothered coming home to die
But simply stayed away out there
In the clean war, the war in the air.

Seldom the ghosts came back bearing their tales
Of hitting the earth, the incompressible sea,

But stayed up there in the relative wind,
Shades fading in the mind,

Who had no graves but only epitaphs
Where never so many spoke for never so few:
Per ardua, said the partisans of Mars,
Per aspera, to the stars.

That was the good war, the war we won
As if there were no death, for goodness' sake,
With the help of the losers we left out there
In the air, in the empty air.

IFF

1.

Hate Hitler? No, I spared him hardly a thought.
But Corporal Irmin, first, and later on
The O.C. (Flying), Wing Commander Briggs,
And the station C.O. Group Captain Ormery—
Now there were men were objects fit to hate,
Hitler a moustache and a little curl
In the middle of his forehead, whereas these
Bastards were bastards in your daily life,
With Power in their pleasure, smile or frown.

2.

Not to forget my navigator Bert,
Who shyly explained to me that the Jews

Were ruining England and Hitler might be wrong
But he had the right idea . . . We were a crew,
And went on so, the one pair left alive
Of a dozen that chose each other flipping coins
At the OTU, but spoke no civil word
Thereafter, beyond the words that had to do
With the drill for going out and getting back.

3.

One night, with a dozen squadrons coming home
To Manston, the tower gave us orbit and height
To wait our turn in their lofty waiting-room,
And on every circuit, when we crossed the Thames,
Our gunners in the estuary below
Loosed off a couple of dozen rounds on spec,
Defending the Commonwealth as detailed to do,
Their lazy lights so slow, then whipping past.
All the above were friends. And then the foe.

HAYDEN CARRUTH | b. 1921

On a Certain Engagement South of Seoul

A long time, many years, we've had these wars.
When they were opened, one can scarcely say.
We were high school students, no more than
    sophomores,

When Italy broke her peace on a dark day,
And that was not the beginning. The following years
Grew crowded with destruction and dismay.

When I was nineteen, once the surprising tears
Stood in my eyes and stung me, for I saw
A soldier in a newsreel clutch his ears

To hold his face together. Those that paw
The public's bones to eat the public's heart
Said far too much, of course. The sight, so raw

And unbelievable, of people blown apart
Was enough to change us without that bark and whine.
We grew disconsolate. Each had his chart

To mark on the kitchen wall the battle-line,
But many were out of date. The radio
Droned through the years, a faithful anodyne.

Yet the news of this slight encounter somewhere below
Seoul stirs my remembrance: we were a few,
Sprawled on the stiff grass of a small plateau,

Afraid. No one was dead. But we were new—
We did not know that probably none would die.
Slowly, then, all vision went askew.

My clothing was outlandish; earth and sky
Were metallic and horrible. We were unreal,
Strange bodies and alien minds; we could not cry

For even our eyes seemed to be made of steel;
Nor could we look at one another, for each
Was a sign of fear, and we could not conceal

Our hatred for our friends. There was no speech.
We sat alone, all of us, trying to wake
Some memory of the selves beyond our reach.

That place was conquered. The nations undertake
Another campaign now, in another land,
A stranger land perhaps. And we forsake

The miseries there that we can't understand
Just as we always have. Yet still my glimpse
Of a scene on the distant field can make my hand

Tremble again. How quiet we are. One limps,
One cannot walk at all, or one is all right,
But one has this experience that crimps

Forgetfulness, especially at night.
Is this a bond? Does this make us brothers?
Or does it bring our hatred back? I might

Have known, but now I do not know. Others
May know. I know when I walk out-of-doors
I have a sorrow not wholly mine, but another's.

JOHN PAUKER | 1921–1991

Jethro Somes' Apostrophe
to His Former Comrades

Able Baker Charlie Dog
Gents I spent some months among
Bless the hollow of this log
This is where my frame was flung

Easy Fox George How
This is where my bones were thrown
But I bear no rancor now
Bless the throwers bless each bone

Bless my wife bless my son
Bless my lonely billiard cue
Bless my anti-aircraft gun
Which may well be lonely too

    *

Matthew keep your halo on
Blow your nose and dry your tears
Same to you Mark Luke and John
I am prayed for by my peers

RICHARD WILBUR | b. 1921

Mined Country

They have gone into the gray hills quilled with birches,
Drag now their cannon up the chill mountains;
But it's going to be long before
Their war's gone for good.

I tell you it hits at childhood more than churches
Full up with sky or buried town fountains,
Rooms laid open or anything
Cut stone or cut wood,

Seeing the boys come swinging slow over the grass
(Like playing pendulum) their silver plates,
Stepping with care and listening
Hard for hid metal's cry.

It's rightly-called-chaste Belphoebe some would miss,
Some, calendar colts at Kentucky gates;
But the remotest would guess that
Some scheme's gone awry.

Danger is sunk in the pastures, the woods are sly,
Ingenuity's covered with flowers!
We thought woods were wise but never
Implicated, never involved.

Cows in mid-munch go splattered over the sky;
Roses like brush-whores smile from bowers;
Shepherds must learn a new language; this
Isn't going to be quickly solved.

Sunshiny field grass, the woods floor, are so mixed up
With earliest trusts, you have to pick back
Far past all you have learned, to go
Disinherit the dumb child,

Tell him to trust things alike and never to stop
Emptying things, but not let them lack
Love in some manner restored; to be
Sure the whole world's wild.

First Snow in Alsace

The snow came down last night like moths
Burned on the moon; it fell till dawn,
Covered the town with simple cloths.

Absolute snow lies rumpled on
What shellbursts scattered and deranged,
Entangled railings, crevassed lawn.

As if it did not know they'd changed,
Snow smoothly clasps the roofs of homes
Fear-gutted, trustless and estranged.

The ration stacks are milky domes;
Across the ammunition pile
The snow has climbed in sparkling combs.

You think: beyond the town a mile
Or two, this snowfall fills the eyes
Of soldiers dead a little while.

Persons and persons in disguise,
Walking the new air white and fine,
Trade glances quick with shared surprise.

At children's windows, heaped, benign,
As always, winter shines the most,
And frost makes marvelous designs.

The night guard coming from his post,
Ten first-snows back in thought, walks slow
And warms him with a boyish boast:

He was the first to see the snow.

Place Pigalle

Now homing tradesmen scatter through the streets
Toward suppers, thinking on improved conditions,
While evening, with a million simple fissions,
Takes up its warehouse watches, storefront beats,
By nursery windows its assigned positions.

Now at the corners of the Place Pigalle
Bright bars explode against the dark's embraces;
The soldiers come, the boys with ancient faces,
Seeking their ancient friends, who stroll and loll
Amid the glares and glass: electric graces.

The puppies are asleep, and snore the hounds;
But here wry hares, the soldier and the whore,
Mark off their refuge with a gaudy door,
Brazen at bay, and boldly out of bounds:
The puppies dream, the hounds superbly snore.

Ionized innocence: this pair reclines,
She on the table, he in a tilting chair,
With Arden ease; her eyes as pale as air
Travel his priestgoat face; his hand's thick tines
Touch the gold whorls of her Corinthian hair.

"Girl, if I love thee not, then let me die;
Do I not scorn to change my state with kings?
Your muchtouched flesh, incalculable, which wrings
Me so, now shall I gently seize in my
Desperate soldier's hands which kill all things."

JAMES DICKEY | 1923–1997

The Firebombing

*Denke daran, dass nach den grossen Zerstörungen
Jedermann beweisen wird, dass er unschuldig war.—Günter Eich*

Or hast thou an arm like God?—The Book of Job

Homeowners unite.

All families lie together, though some are burned alive.
The others try to feel
For them. Some can, it is often said.

Starve and take off

Twenty years in the suburbs, and the palm trees
        willingly leap
Into the flashlights,
And there is beneath them also
A booted crackling of snailshells and coral sticks.
There are cowl flaps and the tilt cross of propellers,
The shovel-marked clouds' far sides against the moon,
The enemy filling up the hills
With ceremonial graves. At my somewhere among
        these,

Snap, a bulb is tricked on in the cockpit

And some technical-minded stranger with my hands
Is sitting in a glass treasure-hole of blue light,
Having potential fire under the undeodorized arms
Of his wings, on thin bomb-shackles,
The "tear-drop-shaped" 300-gallon drop-tanks
Filled with napalm and gasoline.

Thinking forward ten minutes
From that, there is also the burst straight out
Of the overcast into the moon; there is now
The moon-metal-shine of propellers, the quarter-
moonstone, aimed at the waves,
Stopped on the cumulus.

There is then this re-entry
Into cloud, for the engines to ponder their sound.
In white dark the aircraft shrinks; Japan

Dilates around it like a thought.
Coming out, the one who is here is over
Land, passing over the all-night grainfields,
In dark paint over
The woods with one silver side,
Rice-water calm at all levels
Of the terraced hill.
                        Enemy rivers and trees
Sliding off me like snakeskin,
Strips of vapor spooled from the wingtips
Going   invisible   passing   over   on
Over   bridges   roads for nightwalkers

Sunday night in the enemy's country   absolute
Calm   the moon's face   coming   slowly
About
            the inland sea
Slants   is woven with wire thread
Levels out   holds together like a quilt
Off the starboard wing   cloud flickers
At my glassed-off forehead   the moon's now and again
Uninterrupted face going forward
Over the waves in a glide-path
Lost into land.

Going: going with it

Combat booze by my side in a cratered canteen,
Bourbon frighteningly mixed
With GI pineapple juice,
Dogs trembling under me for hundreds of miles,
        on many
Islands, sleep-smelling that ungodly mixture
Of napalm and high-octane fuel,
Good bourbon and GI juice.

Rivers circling behind me around
Come to the fore, and bring
A town with everyone darkened.
Five thousand people are sleeping off
An all-day American drone.
Twenty years in the suburbs have not shown me
Which ones were hit and which not.

Haul on the wheel   racking slowly
The aircraft blackly around
In a dark dream   that   this is
That is like flying inside someone's head

Think of this   think of this

I did not think of my house
But think of my house now

Where the lawn mower rests on its laurels
Where the diet exists
For my own good   where I try to drop
Twenty years, eating figs in the pantry
Blinded by each and all
Of the eye-catching cans that gladly have caught my
    wife's eye
Until I cannot say
Where the screwdriver is   where the children
Get off the bus   where the fly
Hones his front legs   where the hammock folds
Its erotic daydreams   where the Sunday
School text for the day has been put   where the fire
Wood is   where the payments
For everything under the sun
Pile peacefully up,

But in this half-paid-for pantry
Among the red lids that screw off
With an easy half-twist to the left
And the long drawers crammed with dim spoons,

I still have charge—secret charge—
Of the fire developed to cling
To everything: to golf carts and fingernail
Scissors as yet unborn   tennis shoes
Grocery baskets   toy fire engines
New Buicks stalled by the half-moon
Shining at midnight on crossroads   green paint
Of jolly garden tools   red Christmas ribbons:

Not atoms, these, but glue inspired
By love of country to burn,
The apotheosis of gelatin.

Behind me having risen the Southern Cross
Set up by chaplains in the Ryukyus—
Orion, Scorpio, the immortal silver
Like the myths of king-
insects at swarming time—
One mosquito, dead drunk
On altitude, drones on, far under the engines,
And bites between
The oxygen mask and the eye.
The enemy-colored skin of families
Determines to hold its color
In sleep, as my hand turns whiter
Than ever, clutching the toggle—
The ship shakes   bucks
Fire hangs   not yet fire
In the air above Beppu
For I am fulfilling

An "anti-morale" raid upon it.
All leashes of dogs
Break under the first bomb, around those
In bed, or late in the public baths: around those
Who inch forward on their hands
Into medicinal waters.
Their heads come up with a roar
Of Chicago fire:
Come up with the carp pond showing
The bathhouse upside down,
Standing stiller to show it more
As I sail artistically over
The resort town followed by farms,
Singing and twisting
All the handles in heaven   kicking
The small cattle off their feet
In a red costly blast
Flinging jelly over the walls
As in a chemical war-
fare field demonstration.
With fire of mine like a cat

Holding onto another man's walls,
My hat should crawl on my head
In streetcars, thinking of it,
The fat on my body should pale.

Gun down
The engines, the eight blades sighing
For the moment when the roofs will connect
Their flames, and make a town burning with all
American fire.

Reflections of houses catch;
Fire shuttles from pond to pond
In every direction, till hundreds flash with one death.
With this in the dark of the mind,
Death will not be what it should;
Will not, even now, even when
My exhaled face in the mirror
Of bars, dilates in a cloud like Japan.
The death of children is ponds
Shutter-flashing; responding mirrors; it climbs
The terraces of hills
Smaller and smaller, a mote of red dust
At a hundred feet; at a hundred and one it goes out.
That is what should have got in
To my eye

And shown the insides of houses, the low tables
Catch fire from the floor mats,
Blaze up in gas around their heads
Like a dream of suddenly growing
Too intense for war. Ah, under one's dark arms
Something strange-scented falls—when those on earth
Die, there is not even sound;
One is cool and enthralled in the cockpit,
Turned blue by the power of beauty,
In a pale treasure-hole of soft light
Deep in aesthetic contemplation,
Seeing the ponds catch fire
And cast it through ring after ring
Of land: O death in the middle
Of acres of inch-deep water!   Useless

Firing   small arms
Speckles   from the river
Bank   one ninety-millimeter
Misses   far down   wrong petals   gone

It is this detachment,
The honored aesthetic evil,
The greatest sense of power in one's life,
That must be shed in bars, or by whatever
Means, by starvation
Visions in well-stocked pantries:
The moment when the moon sails in between
The tail-booms   the rudders nod   I swing
Over   directly over the heart
The *heart* of the fire. A mosquito burns out on my
    cheek
With the cold of my face   there are the eyes
In blue light   bar light
All masked but them   the moon
Crossing from left to right   in the streams below
Oriental fish form quickly
In the chemical shine,
In their eyes one tiny seed
Of deranged, Old Testament light.

Letting go   letting go
The plane rises gently   dark forms
Glide off me   long water   pales
In safe zones   a new cry enters
The voice box of chained family dogs

We buck   leap over something
Not there   settle back
Leave it   leave it clinging and crying
It consumes them in a hot
Body-flash, old age or menopause
Of children, clings and burns
                                        eating through
And when a reed mat catches fire
From me, it explodes through field after field
Bearing its sleeper   another

Bomb finds a home
And clings to it like a child. And so

Goodbye to the grassy mountains
To cloud streaming from the night engines
Flags   pennons   curved silks
Of air   myself streaming also
My body covered
With flags, the air of flags
Between the engines.
Forever I do sleep in that position,
Forever in a turn
For home that breaks out streaming banners
From my wingtips,
Wholly in position to admire.

O then I knock it off
And turn for home over the black complex thread
        worked through
The silver night-sea,

Following the huge, moon-washed steppingstones
Of the Ryukyus south,
The nightgrass of mountains billowing softly
In my rising heat.
                    Turn and tread down
The yellow stones of the islands
To where Okinawa burns,
Pure gold, on the radar screen,
Beholding, beneath, the actual island form
In the vast water-silver poured just above solid ground,
An inch of water extending for thousands of miles
Above flat ploughland. Say "down," and it is done.

All this, and I am still hungry,
Still twenty years overweight, still unable
To get down there or see
What really happened.
                        But it may be that I could not,
If I tried, say to any
Who lived there, deep in my flames: say, in cold
Grinning sweat, as to another
Of these homeowners who are always curving
Near me down the different-grassed street: say
As though to the neighbor
I borrowed the hedge-clippers from
On the darker-grassed side of the two,
Come in, my house is yours, come in
If you can, if you
Can pass this unfired door. It is that I can imagine
At the threshold nothing
With its ears crackling off

Like powdery leaves,
Nothing with children of ashes, nothing not
Amiable, gentle, well-meaning,
A little nervous for no
Reason   a little worried   a little too loud
Or too easygoing   nothing I haven't lived with
For twenty years, still nothing not as
American as I am, and proud of it.

Absolution? Sentence? No matter;
The thing itself is in that.

ALAN DUGAN | b. 1923

Memorial Service for the Invasion Beach Where the Vacation in the Flesh Is Over

I see that there it is on the beach. It is
ahead of me and I walk toward it: its
following vultures and contemptible dogs
are with it, and I walk toward it. If,
in the approach to it, I turn my back
to it, then I walk backwards: I
approach it as a limit. Even if I fall
to hands and knees, I crawl to it.
Backwards or forwards I approach it.

There is the land on one hand, rising, and
the ocean on the other, falling away;
what the sky does, I can not look to see,
but it's around, as ever, all around.
The courteous vultures move away in groups
like functionaries. The dogs circle and stare
like working police. One wants a heel
and gets it. I approach it, concentrating so
on not approaching it, going so far away
that when I get there I am sideways like
the crab, too limited by carapace to say:

"Oh here I am arrived, all; yours today."
No: kneeling and facing away, I will

fall over backwards in intensity of life
and lie convulsed, downed struggling,
sideways even, and should a vulture ask
an eye as its aperitif, I grant it,
glad for the moment wrestling by a horse
whose belly has been hollowed from the rear,
who's eyeless. The wild dog trapped in its ribs
grins as it eats its way to freedom. Not
conquered outwardly, and after rising once,
I fall away inside, and see the sky around
rush out away into the vulture's craw
and barely can not hear them calling, "Here's one."

Portrait from the Infantry

He smelled bad and was red-eyed with the miseries
of being scared while sleepless when he said
this: "I want a private woman, peace and quiet,
and some green stuff in my pocket. Fuck
the rest." Pity the underwear and socks,
long burnt, of an accomplished murderer,
oh God, of germans and replacements, who
refused three stripes to keep his B.A.R.,
who fought, fought not to fight some days
like any good small businessman of war,
and dug more holes than an outside dog
to modify some Freudian's thesis: "No
man can stand three hundred days
of fear of mutilation and death." What he
theorized was a joke: "To keep a tight
asshole, dry socks and a you-deep hole

with you at all times." Afterwards,
met in a sports shirt with a round wife, he was
the clean slave of a daughter, a power brake
and beer. To me, he seemed diminished
in his dream, or else enlarged, who knows?,
by its accomplishment: personal life
wrung from mass issues in a bloody time
and lived out hiddenly. Aside from sound
baseball talk, his only interesting remark
was, in pointing to his wife's belly, "If
he comes out left foot first" (the way
you Forward March!), "I am going to stuff
him back up." "Isn't he awful?" she said.

Self-Exhortation on Military Themes

"Courage!" I say. Thus exhorting myself,
I say encouraging words the way the lame
Tyrtaeus was supposed to have been paid
to say them, making marching songs to make
whole Spartans march away in whole faith:

> "Now hear this, you sons
> of Hercules: God is on
> our side, so make believe
> black death is white as day.
> Dress up your hair for war
> as if for girls or boys
> and throw your bodies away:
> Love and your death are equal joys."

But in his own crippled song to himself,
"On Marching Lamely," he paid himself to say:

> "Go it alone, kid.
>   Run your own races.
>   But when they say, 'Shit!'
>   squat and make faces."

All these men later died. His and their fame
goes on in all military routines,
while the counter-song I make him say
of army verse I've said and heard
goes on in enlisted men's latrines.

Stentor and Mourning

Sunday was calm and airy
but artillery over the hill
made us too nervous to like it.
Some private tacked his tin
mirror to a palm tree and shaved,
using his helmet for a bowl
that would not hold
much water Monday night. I wondered,
stretched out in the while,
in the sleepy diarrhea of fear,
why soldiers fear remarks
more than a probable mutilation,
and swore myself someday,
after the important war,

to a rule of disobedience
as the bravest way. Nevertheless,
the captain's football voice,
bully as acne and athlete's foot,
commands as public law,
prussian as gossip or
the discipline of smiles;
just like when Hera rallied the Greeks
as they cried by their ships:
she yelled from Stentor's mouth
and they fought again,
not for Helen and souvenirs
or even the gods' graces, but
for Greek good opinion. Now,
after survivors' Friday,
in the short weekend of peace,
I hear that why we fight
is for a buddy's safety or
for vengeance for his death, but
I hold that most of us
nurture a fear in secret,
by and large, about our states'
power: some of us,
unknown in arms, can be
Patroklos in his onrush or
Akilles in his sulk
against the private feat
of doing as we god-damned please,
or charge a public hill
to an approved early death
under the national aegis.

ANTHONY HECHT | b. 1923

FROM **Rites and Ceremonies**

THE ROOM

>Father, adonoi, author of all things,
>>of the three states,
>the soft light on the barn at dawn,
>>a wind that sings
>in the bracken, fire in iron grates,
>>the ram's horn,
>Furnisher, hinger of heaven, who bound
>>the lovely Pleaides,
>entered the perfect treasuries of the snow,
>>established the round
>course of the world, birth, death and disease
>>and caused to grow
>veins, brain, bones in me, to breathe and sing
>>fashioned me air,
>Lord, who, governing cloud and waterspout,
>>o my King,
>held me alive till this my forty-third year—
>>*in whom we doubt*—
>Who was that child of whom they tell
>>in lauds and threnes?
>whose holy name all shall pronounce
>>Emmanuel,
>which being interpreted means,
>>*"Gott mit uns"*?

I saw it on their belts. A young one, dead,
Left there on purpose to get us used to the sight
When we first moved in. Helmet spilled off, head
Blond and boyish and bloody. I was scared that night.
And the sign was there,
The sign of the child, the grave, worship and loss,
Gunpowder heavy as pollen in winter air,
An Iron Cross.

It is twenty years now, Father. I have come home.
But in the camps, one can look through a huge square
Window, like an aquarium, upon a room
The size of my livingroom filled with human hair.
Others have shoes, or valises
Made mostly of cardboard, which once contained
Pills, fresh diapers. This is one of the places
Never explained.

Out of one trainload, about five hundred in all,
Twenty the next morning were hopelessly insane.
And some there be that have no memorial,
That are perished as though they had never been.
Made into soap.
Who now remembers "The Singing Horses of
     Buchenwald"?
"Above all, the saving of lives," whispered the Pope.
Die Vögelein schweigen im Walde,

But for years the screaming continued, night and day,
And the little children were suffered to come along, too.
At night, Father, in the dark, when I pray,

I am there, I am there. I am pushed through
With the others to the strange room
Without windows; whitewashed walls, cement floor.
Millions, Father, millions have come to this pass,
Which a great church has voted to "deplore."

Are the vents in the ceiling, Father, to let the spirit
     depart?
We are crowded in here naked, female and male.
An old man is saying a prayer. And now we start
To panic, to claw at each other, to wail
As the rubber-edged door closes on chance and choice.
He is saying a prayer for all whom this room shall kill.
"I cried unto the Lord God with my voice,
And He has heard me out His holy hill."

"More Light! More Light!"

for Heinrich Blücher and Hannah Arendt

Composed in the Tower before his execution
These moving verses, and being brought at that time
Painfully to the stake, submitted, declaring thus:
"I implore my God to witness that I have made no
     crime."

Nor was he forsaken of courage, but the death was
     horrible,
The sack of gunpowder failing to ignite.
His legs were blistered sticks on which the black sap
Bubbled and burst as he howled for the Kindly Light.

And that was but one, and by no means one of the
    worst;
Permitted at least his pitiful dignity;
And such as were by made prayers in the name of
    Christ,
That shall judge all men, for his soul's tranquillity.

We move now to outside a German wood.
Three men are there commanded to dig a hole
In which the two Jews are ordered to lie down
And be buried alive by the third, who is a Pole.

Not light from the shrine at Weimar beyond the hill
Nor light from heaven appeared. But he did refuse.
A Lüger settled back deeply in its glove.
He was ordered to change places with the Jews.

Much casual death had drained away their souls.
The thick dirt mounted toward the quivering chin.
When only the head was exposed the order came
To dig him out again and to get back in.

No light, no light in the blue Polish eye.
When he finished a riding boot packed down the earth.
The Lüger hovered lightly in its glove.
He was shot in the belly and in three hours bled to death.

No prayers or incense rose up in those hours
Which grew to be years, and every day came mute
Ghosts from the ovens, sifting through crisp air,
And settled upon his eyes in a black soot.

Still Life

Sleep-walking vapor, like a visitant ghost,
          Hovers above a lake
Of Tennysonian calm just before dawn.
Inverted trees and boulders waver and coast
In polished darkness. Glints of silver break
Among the liquid leafage, and then are gone.

Everything's doused and diamonded with wet.
          A cobweb, woven taut
On bending stanchion frames of tentpole grass,
Sags like a trampoline or firemen's net
With all the glitter and riches it has caught,
Each drop a paperweight of Steuben glass.

No birdsong yet, no cricket, nor does the trout
          Explode in water-scrolls
For a skimming fly. All that is yet to come.
Things are as still and motionless throughout
The universe as ancient Chinese bowls,
And nature is magnificently dumb.

Why does this so much stir me, like a code
          Or muffled intimation
Of purposes and preordained events?
It knows me, and I recognize its mode
Of cautionary, spring-tight hesitation,
This silence so impacted and intense.

As in a water-surface I behold
     The first, soft, peach decree
Of light, its pale, inaudible commands.
I stand beneath a pine-tree in the cold,
Just before dawn, somewhere in Germany,
A cold, wet, Garand rifle in my hands.

Where We Crashed

I was calling airspeed
christ
one-thirty-five and
pancake bam
glass going first
breaking slow
slow dream
breaking
slow
sliding
gas and bombs
sliding
you end
now
here
explode
damn
damn
Steinberg
pilot
should
have found
more sky
you end

here
boom
now
boom
gone
no more
gone
good-bye
bye bye
boom
go boom
piled on
into panel
from behind
off
off
swinging
tire loose
strut caught
slow circle
turn
swinging
ripping
gas and bombs
aluminum
hole open
out
sweet
cheese-eating
jesus
out

clumsy
nothing
fuckass
nothing
shithead
nothing
moldy
cunteyed
bastard
nothing
stuck
shove
him
prick
jump
run
sweet
cheese-eating
jesus
run
gas
bombs
running
rain
faint rain
running
farmer
screaming
something
someone
.45

shoot
get back
shoot him back
gas and bombs
running
Stewart
R.O.
Klamath Falls
out
he's out
on the horizon
running
live
O'Brien
L.A.
broken foot
limping
away
all away
from gas
from bombs
Knapp
ball turret
joking
farmer
yelling
Steinberg
staring gray
and in this grass
I didn't die

Spinazzola: *Quella Cantina Là*

A field of wind gave license for defeat.
I can't explain. The grass bent. The wind
seemed full of men but without hate or fame.
I was farther than that farm where the road
slants off to nowhere, and the field I'm sure
is in this wine or that man's voice. The man
and this canteen were also here
twenty years ago and just as old.

Hate for me was dirt until I woke up
five miles over Villach in a smoke
that shook my tongue. Here, by accident,
the wrong truck, I came back to the world.
This canteen is home-old. A man can walk
the road outside without a song or gun.
I can't explain the wind. The field is east
toward the Adriatic from my wine.

I'd walked from cruel soil to a trout
for love but never from a bad sky
to a field of wind I can't explain.
The drone of bombers going home
made the weather warm. My uniform
turned foreign where the olive trees
throw silver to each other down the hill.

Olive leaves were silver I could spend.
Say wind I can't explain. That field is vital
and the Adriatic warm. Don't our real friends
tell us when we fail? Don't honest fields
reveal us in their winds? Planes and men
once tumbled but the war went on absurd.
I can't explain the wine. This crude bench
and rough table and that flaking plaster—
most of all the long nights make this home.

Home's always been a long way from a friend.
I mix up things, the town, the wind, the war.
I can't explain the drone. Bombers seemed
to scream toward the target, on the let-down
hum. My memory is weak from bombs.
Say I dropped them bad with shaking sight.
Call me German and my enemy the air.

Clouds are definite types. High ones, cirrus.
Cumulus, big fluffy kind, and if with rain,
also nimbus. Don't fly into them.
I can't explain. Somewhere in a gray ball
wind is killing. I forgot the stratus
high and thin. I forget my field
of wind, out there east between
the Adriatic and my second glass of wine.

I'll find the field. I'll go feeble down
the road strung gray like spoiled wine
in the sky. A sky too clear of cloud
is fatal. Trust the nimbus. Trust dark clouds

to rain. I can't explain the sun. The man
will serve me wine until a bomber fleet
lost twenty years comes droning home.

I can't explain. Outside, on the road
that leaves the town reluctantly,
way out the road's a field of wind.

Note from Capri to Richard Ryan
on the Adriatic Floor

Dick, I went back to those rocks today,
the ones we ate on nineteen years ago
a week before you ditched, a damn fool
being brave with land not far away.
I thought of steaks and quotes
from funny men. Two bottles of white wine.

The rocks have changed. Nineteen years
of wave and storm have given them
rough edges and the island rots with stores.
You should have tried for land not fame.
Four others ended with you and your bombardier
went babbling to Bari in restraint.

This is futile. Sharks don't carry notes.
What's your face like now with slow eels
sliding through your eyes? Bones can't glow
through barnacles and green piled dark as flak.

Your seatbelt rots too late. If wings
could bring you up and tricky currents
float you seas and seas to here, I'm not sure
I'd know you or would like your jokes.

Dick, I went back to those rocks today,
and sat there, glaring at the sea.

Arm in Arm

Arm in arm in the Dutch dyke
Were piled both friend and foe
With rifle, helmet, motor-bike:
Step over as you go.

They laid the Captain on a bed
Of gravel and green grass.
The little Dutch girl held his head
And motioned us to pass.

Her busy hands seemed smooth as silk
To a soldier in the sun,
When she gave him a jug of milk
In which his blood did run.

O, had the Captain been around
When trenching was begun,
His bright binoculars had found
The enemy's masked gun!

Beside a Church we dug our holes,
By tombstone and by cross.
They were too shallow for our souls
When the ground began to toss.

Which were the new, which the old dead
It was a sight to ask.
One private found a polished head
And took the skull to task

For spying on us . . . Till along
Driving the clouds like sheep,
Our bombers came in a great throng:
And so we fell asleep.

Carentan O Carentan

Trees in the old days used to stand
And shape a shady lane
Where lovers wandered hand in hand
Who came from Carentan.

This was the shining green canal
Where we came two by two
Walking at combat-interval.
Such trees we never knew.

The day was early June, the ground
Was soft and bright with dew.
Far away the guns did sound,
But here the sky was blue.

The sky was blue, but there a smoke
Hung still above the sea
Where the ships together spoke
To towns we could not see.

Could you have seen us through a glass
You would have said a walk
Of farmers out to turn the grass,
Each with his own hay-fork.

The watchers in their leopard suits
Waited till it was time,
And aimed between the belt and boot
And let the barrel climb.

I must lie down at once, there is
A hammer at my knee.
And call it death or cowardice,
Don't count again on me.

Everything's all right, Mother,
Everyone gets the same
At one time or another.
It's all in the game.

I never strolled, nor ever shall,
Down such a leafy lane.
I never drank in a canal,
Nor ever shall again.

There is a whistling in the leaves
And it is not the wind,
The twigs are falling from the knives
That cut men to the ground.

Tell me, Master-Sergeant,
The way to turn and shoot.

But the Sergeant's silent
That taught me how to do it.

O Captain, show us quickly
Our place upon the map.
But the Captain's sickly
And taking a long nap.

Lieutenant, what's my duty,
My place in the platoon?
He too's a sleeping beauty,
Charmed by that strange tune.

Carentan O Carentan
Before we met with you
We never yet had lost a man
Or known what death could do.

Memories of a Lost War

The guns know what is what, but underneath
In fearful file
We go around burst boots and packs and teeth
That seem to smile.

The scene jags like a strip of celluloid,
A mortar fires,
Cinzano falls, Michelin is destroyed,
The man of tires.

As darkness drifts like fog in from the sea
Somebody says
"We're digging in." Look well, for this may be
The last of days.

Hot lightnings stitch the blind eye of the moon,
The thunder's blunt.
We sleep. Our dreams pass in a faint platoon
Toward the front.

Sleep well, for you are young. Each tree and bush
Drips with sweet dew,
And earlier than morning June's cool hush
Will waken you.

The riflemen will wake and hold their breath.
Though they may bleed
They will be proud a while of something death
Still seems to need.

Old Soldier

A dream of battle on a windy night
Has wakened him. The shadows move once more
With rumors of alarm. He sees the height
And helmet of his terror in the door.

The guns reverberate; a livid arc
From sky to sky lightens the windowpanes

And all his room. The clock ticks in the dark;
A cool wind stirs the curtains, and it rains.

He lies remembering: "That's how it was . . ."
And smiles, and drifts into a youthful sleep
Without a care. His life is all he has,
And that is given to the guards to keep.

On the Ledge

I can see the coast coming near . . .
one of our planes, a Thunderbolt, plunging down
and up again. Seconds later
we heard the rattle of machine guns.

That night we lay among hedgerows.
The night was black. There was thrashing
in a hedgerow, a burst of firing . . .
in the morning, a dead cow.

A plane droned overhead . . .
one of theirs,
diesel, with a rhythmic sound.
Then the bombs came whistling down.

                    *

We were strung out on an embankment
side by side in a straight line,
like infantry in World War One
waiting for the whistle to blow.

The Germans knew we were there
and were firing everything they had,
bullets passing right above.
I knew that in a moment the order would come.

There is a page in Dostoevsky
about a man being given the choice
to die, or to stand on a ledge
through all eternity . . .

alive and breathing the air,
looking at the trees, and sky . . .
the wings of a butterfly
as it drifts from stem to stem.

But men who have stepped off the ledge
know all that there is to know:
who survived the Bloody Angle,
Verdun, the first day on the Somme.

As it turned out, we didn't have to.
Instead, they used Typhoons.
They flew over our heads, firing rockets
on the German positions.

So it was easy. We just strolled
over the embankment,
and down the other side,
and across an open field.

Yet, like the man on the ledge,
I still haven't moved . . .
watching an ant
climb a blade of grass and climb back down.

A Bower of Roses

The mixture of smells—
of Algerian tobacco,
wine barrels, and urine—
I'll never forget it,
he thought, if I live to be a hundred.

And the whores in every street,
and like flies in the bars . . .
Some of them looked familiar:
there was a Simone Simone,
a Veronica.

And some were original,
like the two who stood on a corner,
a brunette with hair like ink
and a platinum blonde,
holding a Great Dane on a leash.

"A monster," said Margot.
"Those two give me the shivers."

The other girls were of the same opinion.
One said, "And, after all,
think what a dog like that must cost to feed."

This was conclusive. They stared out at the street—
there was nothing more to be said.

                    *

When they gave him a pass at the hospital
he would make for the bar in Rue Sainte Apolline
Margot frequented. Sitting in a corner
as though she had been waiting . . .

Like the sweetheart on a postcard
gazing from a bower of roses . . .
"Je t'attends toujours."

For ten thousand francs
she would let him stay the night,
and a thousand for the concièrge.
The maid, too, must have something.

Then, finally, he would be alone with her.
Her face a perfect oval,
a slender neck, brown hair . . .

It surprised him that a girl
who looked delicate in her clothes
was voluptuous when she stood naked.

*

He caught up with the division in Germany,
at Dusseldorf, living in houses
a hundred yards from the Rhine.

Now and then a shell flew over.
For every shell Krupp fired
General Motors sent back four.

Division found some cases of beer,
and cigars, and passed them around—
a taste of the luxury
that was coming. The post-war.

One morning they crossed the Rhine.
Then they were marching through villages
where the people stood and stared.
Then they rode in convoys of trucks
on the autobahns. Deeper in.
The areas on the map of Germany
marked with the swastika kept diminishing,
and then, one day, there were none.

*

They were ordered back to France,
only sixty kilometers from Paris.

Once more he found himself climbing the stairs.
He knocked, and heard footsteps.
"Who is it?"
                    The door opened a crack,
then wide, and he was holding her.
"My God," she said, "chéri,
I never thought to see you again."

That night, lying next to her,
he thought about young women
he had known back in the States
who would not let you do anything.
And a song of the first war . . .
"How Are You Going to Keep Them Down on the
      Farm?
(After They've Seen Paree)."

He supposed this was what life taught you,
that words you thought were a joke,
and applied to someone else,
were real, and applied to you.

The Stoic: For Laura Von Courten

All winter long you listened for the boom
Of distant cannon wheeled into their place.
Sometimes outside beneath a bombers' moon
You stood alone to watch the searchlights trace

Their careful webs against the boding sky,
While miles away on Munich's vacant square
The bombs lunged down with an unruly cry
Whose blast you saw yet could but faintly hear.

And might have turned your eyes upon the gleam
Of a thousand years of snow, where near the clouds
The Alps ride massive to their full extreme,
And season after season glacier crowds

The dark, persistent smudge of conifers.
Or seen beyond the hedge and through the trees
The shadowy forms of cattle on the furze,
Their dim coats white with mist against the freeze.

Or thought instead of other times than these,
Of other countries and of other sights:
Eternal Venice sinking by degrees
Into the very water that she lights;

Reflected in canals, the lucid dome
Of Maria della Salute at your feet,
Her triple spires disfigured by the foam.
Remembered in Berlin the parks, the neat

Footpaths and lawns, the clean spring foliage,
Where just short weeks before, a bomb, unaimed,
Released a frightened lion from its cage,
Which in the mottled dark that trees enflamed

Killed one who hurried homeward from the raid.
And by yourself there standing in the chill
You must, with so much known, have been afraid
And chosen such a mind of constant will,

Which, though all time corrode with constant hurt,
Remains, until it occupies no space,
That which it is; and passionless, inert,
Becomes at last no meaning and no place.

EDWARD FIELD | b. 1924

World War II

It was over Target Berlin the flak shot up our plane
just as we were dumping bombs on the already
    smoking city
on signal from the lead bomber in the squadron.
The plane jumped again and again as the shells burst
    under us
sending jagged pieces of steel rattling through our
    fuselage.
It was pure chance
that none of us got ripped by those fragments.

Then, being hit, we had to drop out of formation
    right away
losing speed and altitude,
and when I figured out our course with trembling hands
    on the instruments
(I was navigator)
we set out on the long trip home to England
alone, with two of our four engines gone
and gas streaming out of holes in the wing tanks.
That morning at briefing
we had been warned not to go to nearby Poland
partly liberated then by the Russians,
although later we learned that another crew in trouble

had landed there anyway,
and patching up their plane somehow,
returned gradually to England
roundabout by way of Turkey and North Africa.
But we chose England, and luckily
the Germans had no fighters to send up after us then
for this was just before they developed their jet.
To lighten our load we threw out
guns and ammunition, my navigation books, all the junk
and, in a long descent, made it over Holland
with a few goodbye fireworks from the shore guns.

Over the North Sea the third engine gave out
and we dropped low over the water.
The gas gauge read empty but by keeping the nose
     down
a little gas at the bottom of the tank sloshed forward
and kept our single engine going.
High overhead, the squadrons were flying home in
     formation
—the raids had gone on for hours after us.
Did they see us down there skimming the waves?
We radioed our final position for help to come
but had no idea if anyone
happened to be tuned in and heard us,
and we crouched together on the floor
knees drawn up and head down
in regulation position for ditching;
listened as the engine stopped, a terrible silence,
and we went down into the sea with a crash,
just like hitting a brick wall,

jarring bones, teeth, eyeballs panicky.
Who would ever think water could be so hard?
You black out, and then come to
with water rushing in like a sinking-ship movie.

All ten of us started getting out of there fast:
there was a convenient door in the roof to climb out by,
one at a time. We stood in line,
water up to our thighs and rising.
The plane was supposed to float for twenty seconds
but with all those flak holes
who could say how long it really would?
The two life rafts popped out of the sides into the water
but one of them only half-inflated
and the other couldn't hold everyone
although they all piled into it, except the pilot,
who got into the limp raft that just floated.
The radio operator and I, out last,
(did that mean we were least aggressive, least likely
      to survive?)
we stood on the wing watching the two rafts
being swept off by waves in different directions.
We had to swim for it.
Later they said the cords holding rafts to plane
broke by themselves, but I wouldn't have blamed them
for cutting them loose, for fear
that by waiting for us the plane would go down
and drag them with it.

I headed for the overcrowded good raft
and after a clumsy swim in soaked heavy flying clothes

got there and hung onto the side.
The radio operator went for the half-inflated raft
where the pilot lay with water sloshing over him,
but he couldn't swim, even with his life vest on,
being from the Great Plains—
his strong farmer's body didn't know
how to wallow through the water properly
and a wild current seemed to sweep him farther off.
One minute we saw him on top of a swell
and perhaps we glanced away for a minute
but when we looked again he was gone—
just as the plane went down sometime around then
when nobody was looking.

It was midwinter and the waves were mountains
and the water ice water.
You could live in it twenty-five minutes
the Ditching Survival Manual said.
Since most of the crew were squeezed on my raft
I had to stay in the water hanging on.
My raft? It was their raft, they got there first so they
          would live.
Twenty-five minutes I had.
Live, live, I said to myself.
You've got to live.
There looked like plenty of room on the raft
from where I was and I said so
but they said no.
When I figured the twenty-five minutes were about up
and I was getting numb,
I said I couldn't hold on anymore,

and a little rat-faced boy from Alabama, one of the
     gunners,
got into the icy water in my place,
and I got on the raft in his.
He insisted on taking off his flying clothes
which was probably his downfall because even wet
     clothes are protection,
and then worked hard, kicking with his legs, and we all
     paddled,
to get to the other raft
and tie them together.
The gunner got in the raft with the pilot
and lay in the wet.
Shortly after, the pilot started gurgling green foam from
     his mouth—
maybe he was injured in the crash against the
     instruments—
and by the time we were rescued,
he and the little gunner were both dead.

That boy who took my place in the water
who died instead of me
I don't remember his name even.
It was like those who survived the death camps
by letting others go into the ovens in their place.
It was him or me, and I made up my mind to live.
I'm a good swimmer,
but I didn't swim off in that scary sea
looking for the radio operator when he was
     washed away.
I suppose, then, once and for all,

I chose to live rather than be a hero, as I still do today,
although at that time I believed in being heroic, in
        saving the world,
even if, when opportunity knocked,
I instinctively chose survival.

As evening fell the waves calmed down
and we spotted a boat, not far off, and signaled with a
        flare gun,
hoping it was English not German.
The only two who cried on being found
were me and a boy from Boston, a gunner.
The rest of the crew kept straight faces.

It was a British air-sea rescue boat:
they hoisted us up on deck,
dried off the living and gave us whisky and put us
        to bed,
and rolled the dead up in blankets,
and delivered us all to a hospital on shore
for treatment or disposal.
None of us even caught cold, only the dead.

This was a minor accident of war:
two weeks in a rest camp at Southport on the Irish Sea
and we were back at Grafton-Underwood, our base,
ready for combat again,
the dead crewmen replaced by living ones,
and went on hauling bombs over the continent of
        Europe,
destroying the Germans and their cities.

JOHN HAINES | b. 1924

Mothball Fleet:
Benicia, California

These massed grey shadows
of a distant war,
anchored among burnt hills.

The chained pitch and sweep of them
streaked with rust,
swinging in the sunlit silence,
hinges of a terrible labor.

Years before the last war
my father and I floated past them
on the Chesapeake:
our oarlocks and quiet voices
sounded in the hollow hulls.

And once again these shadows
crossed between me and the sunlight,
formations under flags of smoke.
They carried men, torpedoes,
sealed orders in weighted sacks,
to join tomorrow
some bleak engagement
I will not see.

They are the moving, the stationary
walls of my time.
They hold within them cries,
cold, echoing spaces.

HARVEY SHAPIRO | b. 1924

Battle Report

1

The Adriatic was no sailor's sea.
We raced above that water for our lives
Hoping the green curve of Italy
Would take us in. Rank, meaningless fire

That had no other object but our life
Raged in the stunned engine. I acquired
From the scene that flickered like a silent film
New perspective on the days of man.

Now the aviators, primed for flight,
Gave to the blue expanse can after can
Of calibers, armored clothes, all
The rich paraphernalia of our war.

Death in a hungry instant took us in.
He touched me where my lifeblood danced
And said, the cold water is an ample grin
For all your twenty years.

Monotone and flawless, the blue sky
Shows to my watching face this afternoon
The chilled signal of our victory.
Again the lost plane drums home.

No violence rode in the glistening chamber.
For the gunner the world was unhinged.
Abstract as a drinker and single
He hunched to his task, the dumb show
Of surgical fighters, while flak, impersonal,
Beat at the floor that he stood on.

The diamond in his eye was fear;
It barely flickered.
From target to target he rode.
The images froze, the flak hardly mattered.
Europe rolled to its murderous knees
Under the sex of guns and cannon.

In an absence of pain he continued,
The oxygen misting his veins like summer.
The bomber's long sleep and the cry of the gunner,
Who knows that the unseen mime in his blood
Will startle to terror,
Years later, when love matters.

My pilot dreamed of death before he died.
That stumbling Texas boy
Grew cold before the end, and told
The bombardier, who told us all.
We worried while we slept.
And when he died, on that dark morning
Over Italy in clouds,
We clapped him into dirt.

We counted it for enmity
That he had fraternized with death.
From hand to hand
We passed in wonderment
The quicksilver of our lives.

4

I turn my rubber face to the blue square
Given me to trace the fighters
As they weave their frost, and see
Within this sky the traffic
Fierce and heavy for the day:
All those who stumbling home at dark
Found their names fixed
Beside a numbered Fort, and heard
At dawn the sirens rattling the night away,
And rose to that cold resurrection
And are now gathered over Italy.

In this slow dream's rehearsal,
Again I am the death-instructed kid,
Gun in its cradle, sun at my back,
Cities below me without sound.
That tensed, corrugated hose
Feeding to my face the air of substance,
I face the mirroring past.
We swarm the skies, determined armies,
To seek the war's end, the silence stealing,
The mind grown hesitant as breath.

War Stories

1.

My father read the World Telegram & Sun.
Sometimes he agreed with Westbrook Pegler.
But he never brought home a Hearst paper
except for the Sunday Journal American
because I was a kid and needed the colored comics—
Maggie and Jiggs, Popeye and Dick Tracy.
All those strips I was to see again in high school
in their porno resurrection, strips
in which even Dagwood had a big erection.
I listened to radio serials every afternoon
from five to six: Buck Rogers in the 25th Century,
Jack Armstrong, the All American Boy.
Each one had a special anthem. Later,
in Sioux Falls, South Dakota, at an army base,
I heard them all again. We were in training
as radio gunners in heavy bombers. It was
midwinter and my group was on the midnight shift,
getting up and marching to class in frigid Dakota dark.
The commanding officer issued a directive:
We weren't singing when we marched as Air Force men
    should—
"Into the air Army Air Force./Into the air pilots true."—
So from now on sing! The night the directive was
    read out,
I was marching in the middle of a squad
when suddenly, all around me, everyone

began to sing: "Who's that little chatterbox,
the one with pretty auburn locks. Who
can it be? It's little Orphan Annie."
And so on through all the songs of all
the serials of my childhood.

2.

These are a conquered people,
said the British sergeant,
putting his hand on my shoulder
at the bar in Foggia, Italy—
this is 1944. He was instructing
me on why I should not tip
the Italian barmaid, as I was doing.
A conquered people. I liked the phrase
because it had the ring of history,
suggested dynasty policy, put
the British empire with the Roman
down the long reach of time.
But in the real world it made
no sense. How did it apply
to the Italian kids who came
to my tent each morning to trade
eggs for cigarettes. Or to the old
Italian lady in town who was teaching
me the language. Or to the girl
in the Air Force rest camp on Capri
I fell in love with Christmas week.
They were hardly a people, much less
conquered. They were living
as I lived, on the bare edge of existence,
hoping to survive the interminable war.

But high above their cities
on my way to Germany to kill the enemy
I was part of that sergeant's fictive world,
part of the bloody story of our century.

3.

We were approaching Berlin
at 23,000 feet, our usual
altitude for bombing. P38s,
looking like flying catamarans,
had accompanied us most of the way—
little friend, little friend—from Italy.
Now, nearing the target, we had P51s.
We knew that when their auxiliary fuel tanks
were jettisoned from their underbellies
and came floating down like silver baubles,
a sky full of them,
enemy fighters would shortly show.
A clear blue light flooded my cabin.
Through my window and hatch
I could see what looked like miles
of Flying Fortresses, the big-assed birds
in their tight formations. Blue all around them,
followed by white contrails. Later,
colored tracers would connect bomber
to enemy fighter, and then the black flack
would spread in the sky, a deadly fungus.
Planes would blossom into flame
in that bewildering sky.
How to believe all that happened,
as in a movie, a tv drama, or some other life.

LUCIEN STRYK | b. 1924

Sniper

An inch to the left
and I'd be twenty years
of dust by now. I can't

walk under trees without
his muzzle tracks me.
He'd hit through branches,

leaves pinned to his shoulders
whistling. We searched him
everywhere—up trunks,

in caves, down pits. Then
one night, his island taken,
he stepped from jungle

shade, leaves still pinned
upon him glistening
in the projector's light,

and tiptoed round to watch
our show, a weary kid
strayed in from trick-or-treat.

KENNETH KOCH | 1925–2002

To Carelessness

You led me to sling my rifle
Over my shoulder when its bayonet was fixed
On Leyte, in the jungle. It hit a hornets' nest
And I fell down
Screaming. The hornets attacked me, and Lonnie,
The corporal, said "Soldier get off your ass!"
Later the same day, I stepped on a booby trap
That was badly wired. You
Had been there too.
Thank you. It didn't explode.

To World War Two

Early on you introduced me to young women in bars
You were large, and with a large hand
You presented them in different cities,
Made me in San Luis Obispo, drunk
On French seventy-fives, in Los Angeles, on
        pousse-cafés.
It was a time of general confusion
Of being a body hurled at a wall.
I didn't do much fighting. I sat, rather I stood, in a
        foxhole.

I stood while the typhoon splashed us into morning.
It felt unusual
Even if for a good cause
To be part of a destructive force
With my rifle in my hands
And in my head
My serial number
The entire object of my existence
To eliminate Japanese soldiers
By killing them
With a rifle or with a grenade
And then, many years after that,
I could write poetry
Fall in love
And have a daughter
And think
About these things
From a great distance
If I survived
I was "paying my debt
To society" a paid
Killer. It wasn't
Like anything I'd done
Before, on the paved
Streets of Cincinnati
Or on the ballroom floor
At Mr. Vathé's dancing class
What would Anne Marie Goldsmith
Have thought of me
If instead of asking her to dance
I had put my BAR to my shoulder

And shot her in the face
I thought about her in my foxhole—
One, in a foxhole near me, has his throat cut during
     the night
We take more precautions but it is night and it is you.
The typhoon continues and so do you.
"I can't be killed—because of my poetry. I have to live
     on in order to write it."
I thought—even crazier thought, or just as crazy—
"If I'm killed while thinking of lines, it will be too corny
When it's reported" (I imagined it would be reported!)
So I kept thinking of lines of poetry. One that came to
     me on the beach on Leyte
Was "The surf comes in like masochistic lions."
I loved this terrible line. It was keeping me alive. My
     Uncle Leo wrote to me,
"You won't believe this, but some day you may wish
You were footloose and twenty on Leyte again." I have
     never wanted
To be on Leyte again,
With you, whispering into my ear,
"Go on and win me! Tomorrow you may not be alive,
So do it today!" How could anyone ever win you?
How many persons would I have had to kill
Even to begin to be a part of winning you?
You were too much for me, though I
Was older than you were and in camouflage. But for you
Who threw everything together, and had all the systems
Working for you all the time, this was trivial. If you
     could use me
You'd use me, and then forget. How else

Did I think you'd behave?
I'm glad you ended. I'm glad I didn't die. Or lose
    my mind.
As machines make ice
We made dead enemy soldiers, in
Dark jungle alleys, with weapons in our hands
That produced fire and kept going straight through
I was carrying one,
I who had gone about for years as a child
Praying God don't let there ever be another war
Or if there is, don't let me be in it. Well, I was in you.
All you cared about was existing and being won.
You died of a bomb blast in Nagasaki, and there were
    parades.

SAMUEL MENASHE | b. 1925

Beachhead

The tide ebbs
From a helmet
Wet sand embeds
From a skull
Sea gulls peck

W. D. SNODGRASS | b. 1926

Ten Days Leave

He steps down from the dark train, blinking; stares
At trees like miracles. He will play games
With boys or sit up all night touching chairs.
Talking with friends, he can recall their names.

Noon burns against his eyelids, but he lies
Hunched in his blankets; he is half awake
But still lacks nerve to open up his eyes;
Supposing it were just his old mistake?

But no; it seems just like it seemed. His folks
Pursue their lives like toy trains on a track.
He can foresee each of his father's jokes
Like words in some old movie that's come back.

He is like days when you've gone some place new
To deal with certain strangers, though you never
Escape the sense in everything you do,
"We've done this all once. Have I been here, ever?"

But no; he thinks it must recall some old film, lit
By lives you want to touch; as if he'd slept
And must have dreamed this setting, peopled it,
And wakened out of it. But someone's kept

His dream asleep here like a small homestead
Preserved long past its time in memory
Of some great man who lived here and is dead.
They have restored his landscape faithfully:

The hills, the little houses, the costumes:
How real it seems! But he comes, wide awake,
A tourist whispering through the priceless rooms
Who must not touch things or his hand might break

Their sleep and black them out. He wonders when
He'll grow into his sleep so sound again.

Returned to Frisco, 1946

We shouldered like pigs along the rail to try
And catch that first gray outline of the shore
Of our first life. A plane hung in the sky
From which a girl's voice sang: ". . . you're home
    once more."

For that one moment, we were dulled and shaken
By fear. What could still catch us by surprise?
We had known all along we would be taken
By hawkers, known what authoritative lies

Would plan us as our old lives had been planned.
We had stood years and, then, scrambled like rabbits
Up hostile beaches; why should we fear this land
Intent on luxuries and its old habits?

A seagull shrieked for garbage. The Bay Bridge,
Busy with noontime traffic, rose ahead.
We would have liberty, the privilege
Of lingering over steak and white, soft bread

Served by women, free to get drunk or fight,
Free, if we chose, to blow in our back pay
On smart girls or trinkets, free to prowl all night
Down streets giddy with lights, to sleep all day,

Pay our own way and make our own selections;
Free to choose just what they meant we should;
To turn back finally to our old affections,
The ties that lasted and which must be good.

Off the port side, through haze, we could discern
Alcatraz, lavender with flowers. Barred,
The Golden Gate, fading away astern,
Stood like the closed gate of your own backyard.

JAMES TATE | b. 1943

The Lost Pilot

for my father, 1922–1944

Your face did not rot
like the others—the co-pilot,
for example, I saw him

yesterday. His face is corn-
mush: his wife and daughter,
the poor ignorant people, stare

as if he will compose soon.
He was more wronged than Job.
But your face did not rot

like the others—it grew dark,
and hard like ebony;
the features progressed in their

distinction. If I could cajole
you to come back for an evening,
down from your compulsive

orbiting, I would touch you,
read your face as Dallas,
your hoodlum gunner, now,

with the blistered eyes, reads
his braille editions. I would
touch your face as a disinterested

scholar touches an original page.
However frightening, I would
discover you, and I would not

turn you in; I would not make
you face your wife, or Dallas,
or the co-pilot, Jim. You

could return to your crazy
orbiting, and I would not try
to fully understand what

it means to you. All I know
is this: when I see you,
as I have seen you at least

once every year of my life,
spin across the wilds of the sky
like a tiny, African god,

I feel dead. I feel as if I were
the residue of a stranger's life,
that I should pursue you.

My head cocked toward the sky,
I cannot get off the ground,
and, you, passing over again,

fast, perfect, and unwilling
to tell me that you are doing
well, or that it was mistake

that placed you in that world,
and me in this; or that misfortune
placed these worlds in us.

BIOGRAPHICAL NOTES

SOURCES AND ACKNOWLEDGMENTS

NOTES

INDEX OF TITLES &
FIRST LINES

BIOGRAPHICAL NOTES

CONRAD AIKEN (1889–1973) Born in Savannah, Georgia. Attended Harvard University, where he formed a close friendship with T. S. Eliot. His first book of poetry, *Earth Triumphant*, was published in 1914. Lived in London during the 1920s; *Selected Poems* (1930) won the Pulitzer Prize and *Collected Poems* (1953) received the National Book Award. Served as poetry consultant at the Library of Congress in 1950.

W. H. AUDEN (1907–1973) Born Wystan Hugh Auden in York, England. Educated at Christ Church College, Oxford. T. S. Eliot helped arrange the publication of his first book of verse, *Poems* (1930). Auden went to Spain during the civil war to write in support of the Republican cause and reported on the early phases of the Sino-Japanese war. He moved to the U.S. in 1939 and became a naturalized citizen in 1946. From May to August 1945 he interviewed civilians in Germany about their reactions to Allied bombing while serving with the Morale Division of the U.S. Strategic Bombing Survey. *The Age of Anxiety* (1947) was awarded the Pulitzer Prize. Collaborated with his partner Chester Kallman on the libretto for Igor Stravinsky's opera *The Rake's Progress*. His literary criticism was collected in

The Enchafèd Flood and *The Dyer's Hand*, and his last volume of poetry, *Thank You, Fog*, was published posthumously in 1974.

BEN BELITT (b. 1911) Born in New York City. Attended the University of Virginia. Published *The Five-Fold Mesh* in 1938, the year he began teaching at Bennington College. Served in the combat film section of the Army Signal Corps during World War II. His collected poems, *This Scribe, My Hand*, appeared in 1998.

JOHN BERRYMAN (1914–1972) Born John Allyn Smith in McAlester, Oklahoma. His father killed himself in 1926, and after his mother remarried, Berryman grew up in New York City. Educated at Columbia University and spent two years at Cambridge University. Received medical deferment from the draft during World War II. His first volume of verse, *Poems*, was published in 1942, shortly before he began teaching at Princeton University; it was followed by *The Dispossessed* (1948) and *Stephen Crane* (1950), a biography. Began teaching at the University of Minnesota in 1955 and won acclaim the following year for *Homage to Mistress Bradstreet*. *77 Dream Songs* (1964) was awarded the Pulitzer Prize; the complete *The Dream Songs* was published in 1969. Berryman committed suicide in Minneapolis by jumping off a bridge over the Mississippi. An autobiographical novel about alcoholism, *Recovery*, was published posthumously in 1973.

EDGAR BOWERS (1924–2000) Born in Rome, Georgia. During World War II he served in the Army Counter Intelligence Corps, and was stationed in Germany at the end of the war. Bowers was educated at the University of North Carolina and Stanford University. His first book of poetry, *The Form of Loss*, was published in 1956; two years later he began teaching at the University of California at Santa Barbara. *For Louis Pasteur* won the Bollingen Prize in 1989.

PETER BOWMAN (1917–1985) Served as a correspondent for *Air Force* magazine during World War II. *Beach Red*, his 1945 verse novel about an amphibious invasion in the Pacific, was made into a film in 1967.

WILLIAM BRONK (1918–1999) Born in Fort Edward, New York, and lived most of his life in nearby Hudson Falls. Educated at Dartmouth College. Served in the army as a lieutenant during World War II. After teaching briefly at Union College, he ran the family lumber business for many years. His first volume of verse, *Light and Dark*, appeared in 1956. *Life Supports: New and Collected Poems* (1982) won the American Book Award.

GWENDOLYN BROOKS (1917–2000) Born in Topeka, Kansas. Attended Woodrow Wilson Junior College in Chicago, where she later made her home. Published her first volume of poetry, *A Street in Bronzeville*, in 1945; it included poems about the treatment of black soldiers during World War II. *Annie Allen* (1949) won the Pulitzer Prize for poetry, the first to be awarded to an African-American. In 1969 her long poem *Riot* was published. Brooks served as poetry consultant at the Library of Congress 1985–86.

CHARLES E. BUTLER (1909–1981) Born in Denver, Colorado. Educated at the University of Chicago and the University of Chicago Library School. Served in the army during World War II and was stationed in England. *Cut Is the Branch* (1945) won the Yale Younger Poets Prize. *Follow Me Ever*, a novel, was published in 1950. Worked for many years as a librarian at Longwood College in Farmville, Virginia.

WITTER BYNNER (1881–1968) Born in Brooklyn, New York. Grew up in Connecticut and Massachusetts. After attending Harvard University, moved to New York City, where he worked as an editor for *McClure's* and began publishing poetry. Taught poetry at Berkeley and traveled to China. Moved in 1922 to New Mexico; traveled in Mexico with D. H. and Frieda Lawrence. Published many collections of poetry including *Indian Earth* (1929) and *Against the Cold* (1940); translations of Chinese poetry collected in *The Jade Mountain* (1929). His poems about World War II appear in *Take Away the Darkness* (1947).

HAYDEN CARRUTH (b. 1921) Born in Waterbury, Connecticut. Educated at the University of North Carolina and the

University of Chicago. Served in the Army Air Forces in Italy in the public relations office of a heavy bomber group. Later became editor of *Poetry*, consulting editor of the *Hudson Review*, and poetry editor of *Harper's*. Taught at Syracuse University, where he directed the creative writing program. First volume of poems, *The Crow and the Heart*, was published in 1959; *Scrambled Eggs and Whiskey* (1996) received the National Book Award. Edited a popular anthology of modern American poetry, *The Voice That Is Great Within Us* (1970).

JOHN CIARDI (1916–1986) Born in Boston, Massachusetts. Studied at Tufts University and the University of Michigan. *Homeward to America*, his first volume of poetry, appeared in 1940. Served in the Army Air Forces and flew 16 combat missions over Japan as a gunner in a B-29 before being assigned to write medal commendations and letters of condolence. Taught at Harvard University and at Rutgers University, where he directed the creative writing program. Ciardi was poetry editor of the *Saturday Review* for over 20 years, and hosted the television program *Accent* and the radio show *A Word in Your Ear*. In addition to writing several books of poetry for adults and young readers, he edited the anthology *Mid-Century American Poets* (1950), and his translation of Dante's *Divine Comedy* (1977) received wide acclaim. *Saipan: The War Diary of John Ciardi* was published posthumously in 1988.

ANN DARR (b. 1920) Educated at the University of Iowa. Worked as a copywriter for NBC Radio's *The Woman of Tomorrow*. From 1943 to 1945 she served as a Women's Air Force Service Pilot (WASP), doing precision flying and aircraft testing for the Army Air Forces. A recipient of the Discovery Award from the New York Poetry Center in 1970, Darr has taught at American University. Her collections of poetry include *Do You Take This Woman* (1986) and *Confessions of a Skewed Romantic* (1993).

JAMES DICKEY (1923–1997) Born in Atlanta, Georgia. Enlisted in the Army Air Forces and served as a radar observer in a P-61 fighter-bomber, flying 38 combat missions from the Philippines and Okinawa in 1945. Later served as a navigation instructor during the Korean War. Studied at Vanderbilt University, then wrote copy for advertising agencies in New York City and Atlanta for several years. His first volume of poetry, *Into the Stone*, was published in 1960; *Buckdancer's Choice* (1965) won the National Book Award. Dickey was poetry consultant at the Library of Congress from 1966 to 1968, and in 1969 was appointed poet-in-residence and professor of English at the University of South Carolina. Wrote the best-selling novel *Deliverance* (1970), and later published *Alnilam* (1987) and *To the White Sea* (1993), novels with World War II aviation backgrounds. His collected poems were published in 1993 as *The Whole Motion*.

H. D. (HILDA DOOLITTLE) (1886–1961) Born in Bethlehem, Pennsylvania. Attended Bryn Mawr College. At the suggestion of her close friend Ezra Pound, adopted the pen name H. D. Moved to London, where she married Richard Aldington. Her first book of poetry, *Sea Garden*, was published in 1916. Lived in Switzerland during the 1920s with her daughter, Perdita, and her companion, the novelist Bryher (Annie Winnifred Ellerman). Began psychoanalysis with Sigmund Freud in 1933. Her experiences in London during the 1940–41 Blitz became the basis for *The Walls Do Not Fall* (1944), the first volume of a poetic trilogy completed by *Tribute to the Angels* (1945) and *The Flowering of the Rod* (1946).

ALAN DUGAN (b. 1923) Born in Brooklyn, New York. Attended Queens College before being drafted; served as an aircraft mechanic with the Army Air Forces in the Marianas. Completed his education at Mexico City College, and then worked in advertising and publishing in New York City. *Poems* (1961) received the Yale Younger Poets Prize, the National Book Award, and the Pulitzer Prize. *Poems 7: New and Complete Poetry*, published in 2001, also received the National Book Award.

ROBERT DUNCAN (1919–1988) Born Edward Howard Duncan in Oakland, California, and raised by adoptive parents after his mother died. Began writing poetry as a teenager; attended the University of California for two years. Served as editor of the *Experimental Review* based in Woodstock, New York. Drafted in 1941 but was given a psychiatric discharge when he declared his homosexuality. His first book of poems, *Heavenly City, Earthly City*, was published in 1947. Later volumes included *The Opening of the Field* (1960), *Roots and Branches* (1964), *Bending the Bow* (1968), *Ground Work* (1984), and *Ground Work II* (1987).

RICHARD EBERHART (b. 1904) Born in Austin, Minnesota. Educated at Dartmouth College, St. John's College, Cambridge, and Harvard University. His book-length poem, *A Bravery of Earth*, appeared in 1930, and his collection of verse, *Reading the Spirit*, was published in 1936. Served in the U.S. Navy during World War II as an aerial gunnery instructor. Taught at Dartmouth from 1956 to 1980, and was poetry consultant at the Library of Congress, 1959–61. *Selected Poems* (1965) was awarded the Pulitzer Prize.

WILLIAM EVERSON (1912–1994) Born in Sacramento, California. Attended Fresno State College. First book of poetry, *These Are the Ravens*, was published in 1935. Everson did forestry work in Oregon during World War II after being classified a conscientious objector. In 1951 he entered the Dominican order of the Roman Catholic Church as a lay monk, and published ten volumes of poetry under the name Brother Antoninus. After leaving the order in 1969, he was poet-in-residence at the University of California at Santa Cruz. Continued to publish poetry, including *The Engendering Flood* (1990), the first part of a verse autobiography (never completed).

EDWARD FIELD (b. 1924) Born in Brooklyn, New York, and grew up on Long Island. Attended New York University. Served as a heavy bomber navigator with the Army Air Forces and flew 25 combat missions over northwest Europe. His first book of verse, *Stand Up, Friend, With Me* (1963), won the Lamont Poetry Award of the Academy of American Poets. Began teaching workshops at the Poetry Center of the YMHA in New York City in the 1960s. Co-edited the anthology *A New Geography of Poets* (1992), and in 1993 received the Lambda Literary Award in Poetry.

ROBERT FITZGERALD (1910–1985) Born in Geneva, New York. Educated at Harvard University and Trinity College, Cambridge. Wrote for the New York *Herald-Tribune* and *Time* during the 1930s. Served as a naval officer on the staff of Admiral Chester Nimitz, commander of the Pacific fleet, in Hawaii and Guam. Taught at Sarah Lawrence College and Princeton University, and then lived in Italy for more than a decade before becoming Boylston Professor of Rhetoric at Harvard in 1965. His numerous translations include *The Odyssey* (1961), *The Iliad* (1974), and *The Aeneid* (1983); his own poetry was collected in *Poems* (1935), *A Wreath for the Sea* (1943), *In the Rose of Time* (1956), and *Spring Shade* (1971).

WOODY GUTHRIE (1912–1967) Born Woodrow Wilson Guthrie in Okemah, Oklahoma. Began composing songs about the Dust Bowl in 1935. Moved in 1937 to California, where he performed on KFVD radio in Los Angeles, sang at Communist Party gatherings, and wrote for the newspapers *The Light* and *People's World*. In 1940 he moved to New York City, where he sang on CBS radio shows, released the album *Dust Bowl Ballads*, and wrote for the *Daily Worker*. Toured with the Almanac Singers, folk group founded by Pete Seeger. Wrote autobiography, *Bound for Glory* (1943). Made three voyages with the Merchant Marine in 1943 and served in the Army for several months in 1945. Diagnosed with Huntington's Chorea in 1952, he spent much of the remainder of his life in hospitals.

JOHN HAINES (b. 1924) Born in Norfolk, Virginia. Served in the navy as a radar operator on a destroyer in the Pacific and participated in the Okinawa campaign. Attended art schools in

Washington, D.C., and New York City. Moved in 1947 to Alaska, where he homesteaded in the wilderness for over a decade. His first volume of verse, *Winter News*, was published in 1966. Haines was poet-in-residence at the University of Alaska, the University of Washington, and the University of Montana. *New Poems* (1990) received the Western States Book Award. Recent publications include *Fables and Distances* (1996), a book of essays, and *At the End of This Summer* (1997), a collection of poems.

ALFRED HAYES (1911–1985) Born in London, England. Immigrated to the U.S. at the age of two and grew up in New York City, where he attended City College. Early poem "Joe Hill" later became the lyric of a labor ballad with music by Earl Robinson. During World War II Hayes was a member of an Army Special Services (entertainment) unit in Italy. His first book of poetry, *The Big Time*, appeared in 1944. Following the war Hayes stayed in Italy, where he worked on film scripts, including Rossellini's *Paisan*, and wrote novels, including *The Girl on the Via Flaminia*. Settled in California and wrote more fiction and poetry as well as screenplays and teleplays.

ANTHONY HECHT (b. 1923) Born in New York City. Educated at Bard College. Served in the 97th Infantry Division as a rifleman and saw combat in Germany and Czechoslovakia in 1945; participated in the liberation of Flossenberg concentration camp. Later served in the occupation of Japan. After graduate study at Columbia University, taught at Smith College, Bard College, the University of Rochester, and Georgetown University. First book of poetry, *A Summoning of Stones*, was published in 1954. *The Hard Hours* (1967) was awarded the Pulitzer Prize. Served as chancellor of the Academy of American Poets from 1971 to 1997, as poetry consultant at the Library of Congress from 1982 to 1984, and received the Bollingen Prize in 1983. *The Darkness and the Light*, a collection of poems, appeared in 2001.

RICHARD HUGO (1923–1982) Born Richard Hogan in Seattle, Washington. Abandoned by his father as a young child, he grew up with his maternal grandparents. Began to use his stepfather's name when he was in high school. Served with the Army Air Forces in Italy, flying 35 combat missions over central Europe as a B-24 bombardier. Educated at the University of Washington. Worked for Boeing as an industrial writer. *A Run of Jacks*, his first published book of poems, appeared in 1961; *Good Luck in Cracked Italian* (1969) contains a number of poems about World War II. Taught at the University of Montana, where he directed the creative writing program, and was poet-in-residence at the University of Iowa, the University of Washington, and the University of Colorado.

RANDALL JARRELL (1914–1965) Born in Nashville, Tennessee. Spent parts of his childhood in Southern California. Educated at Vanderbilt University, where he associated with the Fugitive group of writers, including John Crowe Ransom, Allen Tate, and Robert Penn Warren. Taught at Kenyon College and the University of Texas, and wrote poetry reviews for *The New Republic*. His first volume of poems, *Blood for a Stranger*, was published in 1942. During World War II Jarrell served in the Army Air Forces, teaching celestial navigation at bases in the U.S. *Little Friend, Little Friend* (1945) and *Losses* (1948) included poems about the air war based on personal encounters with fliers and combat reports. Taught at Sarah Lawrence College and at the University of North Carolina at Greensboro. Wrote *Pictures from an Institution* (1954), a satirical novel about academia. Served as poetry consultant at the Library of Congress, 1957–58. *The Woman at the Washington Zoo* (1960), a collection of poems and translations, won the National Book Award. Jarrell died when he was struck by a car.

ROBINSON JEFFERS (1887–1962) Born in Pittsburgh, Pennsylvania. Educated at Occidental College and the University of Southern California. Early poems were privately published as *Flagons and Apples* (1912). Built a rambling stone house overlooking the Pacific Ocean in Carmel, California, where he wrote the poems in *Roan Stallion, Tamar, and Other Poems* (1925), *Cawdor* (1928), *Give Your Heart to the Hawks* (1933), and *Be Angry at the Sun* (1941). Poems criticizing U.S. involvement in World War II and attacking American political leaders prompted Jeffers' publisher, Random House, to include a disclaimer in *The Double Axe* (1948).

WELDON KEES (1914–1955?) Born in Beatrice, Nebraska. Attended the University of Nebraska. Worked for the Federal Writers' Project in Lincoln, then moved to Denver. Published short stories. Received draft deferment for medical reasons. Moved in 1943 to New York City, where he worked as a newsreel editor for Paramount and wrote book reviews for *Time*, *The New Republic*, *Partisan Review*, and *The New York Times*. His first volume of poetry, *The Last Man*, was published in 1943. Kees also exhibited his abstract expressionist paintings and wrote art criticism for *The Nation*. Moved in 1950 to San Francisco, where he continued to write and paint while also working as a photographer, jazz composer, experimental filmmaker, and radio host. Suffered increasing bouts of depression; in 1955 his car was found abandoned near the Golden Gate Bridge.

LINCOLN KIRSTEIN (1907–1996) Born in Rochester, New York. Educated at Harvard. Edited *Hound and Horn*, 1927–34. Published his first poetry collection, *Low Ceiling*, in 1935. Co-founded and directed several ballet schools and companies, including American Ballet and Ballet Caravan, and wrote several books about dance. Served in northwest Europe with Third Army headquarters as a courier, driver, and interpreter, and helped search for looted art works after the Nazi surrender. Wrote about his wartime experiences in *Rhymes of a PFC* (1964). Founded the New York City Ballet and served as its general director from 1948 to 1989.

KENNETH KOCH (1925–2002) Born in Cincinnati, Ohio. Served in the Philippines with the 96th Infantry Division as a rifleman and saw combat on Leyte. Educated at Harvard University and at Columbia University, where he taught English. Became closely associated with the poets John Ashbery and Frank O'Hara as well as with abstract expressionist painters. His numerous collections of poetry included *Thank You and Other Poems* (1963), *The Art of Love* (1975), and *Days and Nights* (1982); *On the Great Atlantic Railway* (1994) won the Bollingen Prize. Koch also produced experimental verse plays and wrote books on teaching poetry to children and elderly people.

STANLEY KUNITZ (b. 1905) Born in Worcester, Massachusetts. Educated at Harvard University. Worked as an editor at H. W. Wilson Publishing Company in New York City. His first volume of poems, *Intellectual Things*, appeared in 1930. Served in the Air Transport Command during World War II. *Selected Poems* (1958) won the Pulitzer Prize. Taught at Columbia University from 1963 to 1985. Kunitz was poetry consultant at the Library of Congress, 1974–75. *The Collected Poems* was published in 2000. Kunitz was poet laureate of the United States, 2000–1.

ROBERT LOWELL (1917–1977) Born in Boston, Massachusetts. Attended Harvard University for two years, then completed his undergraduate work at Kenyon College, where he studied with John Crowe Ransom; also studied at Louisiana State University with Cleanth Brooks and Robert Penn Warren. In 1943 Lowell refused to be inducted into the armed forces in protest against the Allied bombing of German cities, the policy of unconditional surrender, and the U.S. alliance with the Soviet Union. Sentenced to a year in prison, he served five months. *Lord Weary's Castle* (1946) won the Pulitzer Prize, *Life Studies* (1959) received the National Book Award, and *Imitations* (1961) was awarded the Bollingen Prize for translation. He adapted stories by Hawthorne and Melville for the stage; the New York City production of *The Old Glory* earned him an Obie Award. In the 1960s Lowell taught at Harvard and was writer-in-residence at Yale; in 1970 he taught at Oxford University. *The Dolphin* (1973) won the Pulitzer Prize for poetry.

THOMAS MCGRATH (1916–1990) Born near Sheldon, North Dakota. Attended the University of North Dakota and Louisiana State University. Published his early poems in *First Manifesto* (1940). After joining the Communist Party, McGrath moved to New York City, where he worked in a shipyard and as a labor organizer. During World War II he served with the Army Air Forces in the Aleutian Islands. Taught at Los Angeles State University from 1951 to 1954, but was dismissed after appearing as an unfriendly witness before the House Un-American Activities Committee. Later taught at North Dakota State University and Moorhead State University, and founded the literary journal *Crazy Horse*.

SAMUEL MENASHE (b. 1925) Born in New York City. Attended Queens College. Served with the 87th Infantry Division in France, Belgium, Luxemburg, and Germany. Studied at the Sorbonne in Paris. His first book of poetry, *The Many Named Beloved*, was published in 1961; *The Niche Narrows* appeared in 2000.

WILLIAM MEREDITH (b. 1919) Born in New York City. Educated at Princeton University and worked as a reporter for *The New York Times*. Served as a naval pilot during World War II, based in the Aleutian Islands and Hawaii; later flew from aircraft carriers during the Korean War. His first volume of poems, *Love Letter from an Impossible Land* (1944), won the Yale Younger Poets Prize. In 1955 he began his long teaching career at Connecticut College. Meredith was also an instructor at the Bread Loaf Writers' Conference and directed the humanities division of the Upward Bound Program. He was poetry consultant at the Library of Congress, 1978–80, and chancellor of the Academy of American Poets from 1963 to 1987. *Partial Accounts* (1987) won the Pulitzer Prize; *Effort at Speech* (1997) received the National Book Award.

MARIANNE MOORE (1887–1972) Born in Kirkwood, Missouri. Grew up in Carlisle, Pennsylvania. Studied at Bryn Mawr College, majoring in biology, and published her first poems in the college literary magazine. Taught business classes and coached athletics at the Indian School in Carlisle. Moved to New York City in 1918, and worked for the New York Public Library and as an editor of *The Dial.* Her *Collected Poems* (1951) won the Bollingen Prize, the National Book Award, and the Pulitzer Prize. Moore spent nine years translating La Fontaine's *Fables* (1954), and collected her essays and reviews in *Predilections* (1955).

VLADIMIR NABOKOV (1899–1977) Born in St. Petersburg, Russia. Family went into exile in 1919. Educated at Trinity College, Cambridge University. Settled in Berlin, publishing stories, poems, and novels in Russian. Left Berlin for Paris in 1937, then immigrated to the United States in 1940. First novel written in English, *The Real Life of Sebastian Knight*, was published in 1941. Taught at Wellesley and several other colleges before taking a position at Cornell University in 1947. American publication of *Lolita* in 1958 brought wide public attention. Moved to Switzerland in 1961. Novel *Pale Fire* (1962) contained a 999-line poem; *Poems and Problems* (1970) collected poems written in English, as well as English versions of his Russian poems.

HOWARD NEMEROV (1920–1991) Born in New York City. Educated at Harvard University. Enlisted in the Royal Canadian Air Force in 1942 and became a pilot flying anti-submarine and anti-shipping patrols for RAF Coastal Command over the North Atlantic and the North Sea. His first book of poems, *The Image and the Law*, was published in 1947. Served as poetry consultant at the Library of Congress, 1963–64, chancellor of the Academy of American Poets, and poet laureate of the United States, 1988–90. Appointed professor of English and poet-in-residence at Washington University in 1969. *Collected Poems* (1977) won the Bollingen Prize, the National Book Award, and the Pulitzer Prize.

JOHN FREDERICK NIMS (1913–1999) Born in Muskegon, Michigan. Educated at Notre Dame University and the University of Chicago, and taught at Notre Dame during World

War II. *The Iron Pastoral* (1947) was his first book of poetry. Taught at the Bread Loaf Writers' Conference, edited *Poetry*, and translated poems of St. John of the Cross and Michelangelo. Edited poetry textbook *Western Wind* (1974).

GEORGE OPPEN (1908–1984) Born George Oppenheimer in New Rochelle, New York. Family moved to San Francisco in 1918. Published poems in the 1931 Objectivist issue of *Poetry*, edited by Louis Zukofsky. Established Objectivist Press with Zukofsky, Charles Reznikoff, and William Carlos Williams. Joined Communist Party in 1935 and worked as a labor organizer for several years. Served in an anti-tank company of the 103rd Infantry Divison in the Vosges, Alsace, and Germany from November 1944 until April 22, 1945, when he was seriously wounded by shellfire. Moved to Mexico in 1950 to avoid FBI investigation and remained there until 1960. After a long hiatus, resumed writing poetry in the early 1960s. *Of Being Numerous* (1968) was awarded the Pulitzer Prize.

JOHN PAUKER (1920–1991) Born in Budapest, Hungary. Immigrated to the United States at the age of four and grew up in New York City. Educated at Yale University. Served in the army during World War II and made broadcasts for the Office of War Information from North Africa and Europe. Later worked for the Voice of America and the United States Information Agency. Pauker was a translator as well as the editor of the literary journal *Furioso*. His poems were collected in *Yoked by Violence* (1949) and *Excellency* (1968).

HYAM PLUTZIK (1911–1962) Born in Brooklyn, New York. Studied at Trinity College and Yale University, and then worked as a newspaper reporter. His first collection of poems, *Death at the Purple Rim*, was published privately in 1941. Served in the Army Air Forces as an ordnance and education officer stationed in England. Later taught at the University of Rochester. His later books of poetry included *Aspects of Proteus* (1949) and *Apples from Shinar* (1959).

EZRA POUND (1885–1972) Born in Hailey, Idaho. Grew up in Philadelphia and was educated at the University of Pennsylvania and Hamilton College. His first volume of poetry, *A Lume Spento*, was published in 1908. Moved to London in 1908 and became a major figure in the modernist movement. Began publishing the poems that would become *The Cantos* in 1916. *Hugh Selwyn Mauberley* appeared in 1920. Settled in Rapallo, Italy, in 1925. Made 120 broadcasts over Italian radio from 1941 to 1943 that were marked by anti-Semitic invective and the vilification of Allied leaders, and was indicted for treason by a federal grand jury in 1943. Surrendered to the U.S. Army in May 1945 and was imprisoned at Pisa before being returned to the United States in November 1945. After being found mentally unfit to stand trial in 1946, Pound was committed to St. Elizabeths Hospital in Washington, D.C. *The Pisan Cantos* (1948) was awarded the Bollingen Prize, causing a major controversy. In 1958 the government agreed to dismiss the treason indictment, and Pound was released from St. Elizabeths and allowed to return to Italy.

CHARLES REZNIKOFF (1894–1976) Born in Brooklyn, New York. Attended New York University Law School. Published poetry collection *Rhythms* (1918) at his own expense; became associated with Objectivist poets including Louis Zukofsky and George Oppen, and published poetry collections including *In Memoriam: 1933* (1934), *Going To and Fro and Walking Up and Down* (1941), and *Inscriptions: 1944–1956* (1959). Many of his books were self-published. His later books included *By the Well of Living and Seeing: New and Selected Poems* (1974) and *Holocaust* (1975), poetry based on testimony from the Nuremberg war crimes trials.

MAY SARTON (1912–1995) Born Eléanore Marie Sarton in Wondelgem, Belgium. Grew up in Cambridge, Massachusetts. In the 1930s she was a theater director in Hartford, Connecticut, and taught writing in Boston. Her first book of verse, *Encounter in April*, was published in 1937. During World War II she was a writer for the Office of War Information. Later became poet-in-residence at Southern Illinois University, taught at Harvard University and Wellesley College, and lectured at the Bread Loaf Writers' Conference. Selected poems published in 1961 as *Cloud, Stone, Sun, Vine*. Moved to York, Maine, in the early 1970s; her later writings included *Journal of a Solitude* (1973) and *Recovering* (1980).

WINFIELD TOWNLEY SCOTT (1910–1968) Born in Haverhill, Massachusetts. Grew up in Newport, Rhode Island. Educated at Brown University. Scott was literary editor of the Providence *Journal* during the 1930s and 1940s. Early collections of his poems included *Wind the Clock* (1941), *The Sword on the Table* (1942), and *To Marry Strangers* (1945). His long poem *The Dark Sister* appeared in 1958. Moved to the Southwest and became literary editor of the Santa Fe *New Mexican*. Later volumes of verse included *Collected Poems* (1962) and *Letter to the World* (1966).

HARVEY SHAPIRO (b. 1924) Born in Chicago, Illinois. Served in the Army Air Force, flying 35 combat missions over central Europe as a B-17 radio gunner based in Italy. Educated at Yale University and Columbia University. Taught at Cornell University in the early 1950s. After working as an editor at *Commentary* and *The New Yorker*, in 1957 Shapiro began a long association with *The New York Times*, holding various editorial positions at the newspaper, serving as the editor of its book review section. His first book of poetry, *The Eye*, appeared in 1953; his most recent collection, *How Charlie Shavers Died and Other Poems*, appeared in 2001.

KARL SHAPIRO (1913–2000) Born in Baltimore. Attended schools in Maryland, Chicago, and Virginia. In 1935 his first book of verse, *Poems*, was published. Served as a medical corps clerk in the South Pacific, mostly on New Guinea. *V-Letter* (1944), written during his military service, won the Pulitzer Prize. He was poetry consultant at the Library of Congress, 1947–48. Shapiro taught at Johns Hopkins University, the University of Nebraska, the University of Chicago, and the University of California at Davis, and edited *Poetry* and *Prairie Schooner.* Shared the Bollingen Prize with John Berryman in 1969. His novel *Edsel* was published in 1971.

LOUIS SIMPSON (b. 1923) Born in Jamaica in the West Indies. Immigrated to the United States in 1940. Served as an infantryman in the 101st Airborne Division in France, Holland, Belgium, and Germany, and was wounded twice. Educated at Columbia University. Worked as an editor at Bobbs-Merrill, then taught at Columbia, the University of California at Berkeley, and the State University of New York at Stony Brook. His first book of verse, *The Arrivistes,* was privately printed in Paris in 1949. *At the End of the Open Road* (1963) was awarded the Pulitzer Prize. More recently he has published *There You Are* (1995). Simpson is also the author of several volumes of nonfiction, memoirs, translations, and a novel.

WILLIAM JAY SMITH (b. 1918) Born in Winnfield, Louisiana. Grew up at Jefferson Barracks, army base outside of St. Louis, Missouri. Attended Washington University. Served in the navy during World War II as a liaison officer onboard Free French ships in the Pacific. Studied in France, England, and Italy. His first book of verse, *Poems,* was published in 1947. Smith was writer-in-residence at Williams College and the Arena Stage in Washington, D. C. Taught at Hollins College and Columbia University, served for one term in the Vermont house of representatives, reviewed poetry for *Harper's,* and served as poetry consultant at the Library of Congress, 1968–70. Smith has written ten several books of verse for children and translated French literature. His most recent book of poetry, *The Cherokee Lottery,* was published in 2000.

W. D. SNODGRASS (b. 1926) Born William DeWitt Snodgrass in Wilkinsburg, Pennsylvania. Attended Geneva College. Served in the navy in the Pacific. Completed his education at the University of Iowa, then taught at Wayne State University,

Syracuse University, and the University of Delaware. His first volume of verse, *Heart's Needle* (1959), was awarded the Pulitzer Prize; *The Fuehrer Bunker: The Complete Cycle* appeared in 1995. Critical essays and lectures were collected in *In Radical Pursuit* (1975). Snodgrass has also translated German, Romanian, and Hungarian songs. His autobiography, *After-Images*, appeared in 1999.

WILLIAM STAFFORD (1914–1993) Born in Hutchinson, Kansas. Studied at the University of Kansas and the University of Iowa. Received conscientious objector status during World War II and worked on forestry and soil conservation projects in Arkansas and California. Taught at Lewis and Clark College for many years. His first volume of poems, *West of Your City*, was published in 1960; *Traveling Through the Dark* (1962) won the National Book Award. Served as poetry consultant at the Library of Congress, 1970–71, and as poet laureate of Oregon.

LUCIEN STRYK (b. 1924) Born in Chicago, Illinois. Served in the army during World War II. Educated at the Sorbonne in Paris, the University of Maryland, and the University of Iowa. Taught at Northern Illinois University and lectured at Japanese universities. In 1953 his first book of verse, *Taproot*, appeared; more recently he has published *And Still the Birds Sing* (1998). Stryk has translated Zen poetry from China and Japan.

ALLEN TATE (1899–1979) Born in Winchester, Kentucky. Attended Vanderbilt University, where he became a member of the Fugitive group of Southern writers. His first poetry collection, *Mr. Pope and Other Poems*, was published in 1928. Co-edited and contributed to the Southern agrarian manifesto *I'll Take My Stand* (1930). Tate was poet-in-residence at Princeton University, 1939–42, and poetry consultant at the Library of Congress, 1943–44. Edited the *Sewanee Review* and became a professor at the University of Minnesota in 1951. Awarded the Bollingen Prize in 1957. *Collected Poems* appeared in 1977.

JAMES TATE (b. 1943) Born in Kansas City, Missouri. His father, a bomber pilot in the Army Air Forces, was killed over Germany in 1944 when Tate was five months old. Tate was educated at Kansas State College and the University of Iowa. Began teaching at the University of Massachusetts in 1971. *The Lost Pilot* (1967) was awarded the Yale Younger Poets Prize; his *Selected Poems* (1991) received the Pulitzer Prize.

EVE TRIEM (1902–1992) Born in New York City. Grew up in San Francisco and attended the University of California at Berkeley. Lived in Seattle, Washington. Her first book of verse, *Parade of Doves*, appeared in 1946; her last volume, *Nobody Dies in Summer*, in 1992.

PETER VIERECK (b. 1916) Born in New York City, son of poet and journalist George Sylvester Viereck. Educated at Harvard. Served in the U.S. Army psychological warfare branch in North Africa and Italy, 1943–44. His brother was killed at Anzio in 1944. His father was convicted in 1942 of serving as a German propaganda agent and was imprisoned until 1947. Viereck was a professor of history at Mount Holyoke College from 1948 to 1987 and published several books on the history of conservative thought. His first book of poetry, *Terror and Decorum* (1948), was awarded the Pulitzer Prize; his most recent volume of verse was *Tide and Continuities* (1995). Viereck has also translated German and Russian poetry.

EDWARD R. WEISMILLER (b. 1915) Born in Monticello, Wisconsin. Lived on a farm in Vermont, where he first began to write poetry. Educated at Cornell College, Merton College, Oxford, and Harvard University. *The Deer Came Down* (1936), his first book of poetry, was awarded the Yale Younger Poets Prize. Joined X-2, the counterintelligence branch of the Office of Strategic Services, in 1943 and served in London, Cherbourg, and Paris as a controller of double agents. Co-wrote a two-volume history of OSS double-agent operations. His volumes of poetry include *The Faultless Shore* (1946), *The Branch of Fire*

(1980), and *Walking Into the Sun* (2002). His novel *The Serpent Sleeping* (1962) drew on his wartime experiences. Taught at Pomona College, 1950–68, and George Washington University, 1968–80, and published critical essays on the poetry of John Milton.

RICHARD WILBUR (b. 1921) Born in New York City. Grew up in North Caldwell, New Jersey. Attended Amherst College. Served in signal company of the 36th Infantry Division in Italy, France, and Germany. His first volume of poetry, *The Beautiful Changes*, was published in 1947. Taught at Harvard, Wellesley, and Wesleyan before beoming writer-in-residence at Smith. *Things of This World* (1956) won the National Book Award and the Pulitzer Prize, *Walking to Sleep* (1969) was awarded the Bollingen Prize, and *New and Collected Poems* (1988) also won the Pulitzer Prize. Wilbur wrote lyrics for Leonard Bernstein's musical adaptation of *Candide* (1956), and his versions of the plays of Molière received a Bollingen Prize for translation. Served as poet laureate of the United States from 1987 to 1988.

YVOR WINTERS (1900–1968) Born in Chicago, Illinois. Raised in Pasadena, California. Educated at the University of Chicago, the University of Colorado, and Stanford University, where he then taught. His early poems appeared in *The Immobile Wind* (1921) and *The Bare Hills* (1927); *Collected Poems* (1960) was awarded the Bollingen Prize in poetry. Published studies of Edwin Arlington Robinson and W. B. Yeats, as well as *In Defense of Reason* (1947) and *The Forms of Discovery* (1967).

LOUIS ZUKOFSKY (1904–1978) Born in New York City. Educated at Columbia University and taught at the University of Wisconsin and at the Polytechnic Institute of Brooklyn. Corresponded with Ezra Pound; edited the 1931 Objectivist issue of *Poetry*, and helped found the Objectivist Press. His long poem *"A"* was published between 1959 and 1975. Other poems were collected in *All: The Collected Short Poems* (1965–66) and *80 Flowers* (1978).

SOURCES AND ACKNOWLEDGMENTS

The following list identifies the source for each of the poems included in this volume and provides copyright information and acknowledgments. Great care has been taken to trace all owners of copyright material included in this book. If any have been inadvertently omitted or overlooked, acknowledgment will gladly be made in future printings.

Witter Bynner, Defeat: *Take Away the Darkness* (New York: Alfred A. Knopf, 1947). Also appeared in *Selected Poems*, edited by Richard Wilbur and published by Farrar, Straus & Giroux. Copyright © 1978 by Witter Bynner. Reprinted with permission of Farrar, Straus & Giroux, LLC.

Ezra Pound, *from* Canto LXXXIII: *The Cantos* (New York: New Directions, 1970, third printing). Copyright © Ezra Pound. Reprinted with permission of New Directions Publishing Corporation and Faber & Faber, Ltd.

H. D., R.A.F.: *Collected Poems 1912–1944*, edited by Louis L. Martz (New York: New Directions, 1983). Copyright © 1982 by The Estate of Hilda Doolittle. Reprinted with permission of New Directions Publishing Corporation.

Robinson Jeffers, Pearl Harbor: *The Selected Poetry of Robinson Jeffers*, edited by Tim Hunt (Stanford, CA: Stanford University Press, 2001). Copyright © 1948 by Robinson Jeffers. Also appeared in *The Double Axe and Other Poems*, published by Liveright in 1977. Reprinted with permission of

(Fayetteville: University of Arkansas Press, 1995). Ripeness Is All: *Terror and Decorum* (New York: Charles Scribner's Sons, 1948). Poems copyright 1948, © 1995 by Peter Viereck and are reprinted with permission of University of Arkansas Press and the author.

Peter Bowman, *from* Beach Red: *Beach Red* (New York: Random House, 1945). Copyright © 1945 by Peter Bowman. Reprinted with permission of Random House, Inc.

Gwendolyn Brooks, Negro Hero: *Selected Poems* (New York: Harper & Row, 1963). Also appeared in *Blacks*, published in 1987 by David Co. Copyright © 1987 by Gwendolyn Brooks Blakely. Reprinted with permission of The Estate of Gwendolyn Brooks.

Robert Lowell, On the Eve of the Feast of the Immaculate Conception: 1942, The Bomber: *Land of Unlikeness* (Cummington, MA: The Cummington Press, 1944). Memories of West Street and Lepke: *Selected Poems* (New York: Farrar, Straus & Giroux, 1976). Poems also appeared in *Collected Poems*, published in 2003 by Farrar, Straus & Giroux. Copyright © 2002 by The Estate of Robert Lowell. Reprinted with permission of Farrar, Straus & Giroux, LLC and Faber & Faber, Ltd.

William Bronk, Soldiers in Death, Memorial: *Life Supports: New and Collected Poems* (San Francisco: North Point Press, 1982). Copyright © 1982 by William Bronk. Reprinted with permission of the William Bronk Papers, Rare Book and Manuscript Library, Columbia University.

William Jay Smith, Epithalamium in Olive Drab, Columbus Circle Swing: *Collected Poems 1939–1989* (New York: Charles Scribner's Sons, 1990). Copyright © 1990 by William Jay Smith. Reprinted with permission of the author. Pidgin Pinch: *Collected Poems 1939–1989* (New York: Charles Scribner's Sons, 1990). Also appeared in *World Beneath the Window: Poems 1937–1997*, published in 1998 by Johns Hopkins University Press. Copyright © 1998 by William Jay Smith. Reprinted with permission of Johns Hopkins University Press.

Robert Duncan, A Spring Memorandum: Fort Knox: *The Years as Catches* (Berkeley: Oyez Press, 1966). Copyright © 1966 by Robert Duncan.

William Meredith, Navy Field: *Effort at Speech* (Evanston, IL: TriQuarterly Books, 1997). Love Letter from an Impossible Land: *Love Letter from an Impossible Land* (New Haven: Yale University Press, 1944). Simile: *Partial Accounts: New and Selected Poems*. All poems copyright © William Meredith and reprinted with permission of the author.

Ann Darr, Flight as a Way of Life: *St. Ann's Gut* (New York: William Morrow & Company, 1971). Copyright © 1971 by Ann Darr. Reprinted with permission.

Howard Nemerov, A Fable of the War, A Memory of the War: *The Collected Poems of Howard Nemerov* (Chicago: University of Chicago Press, 1977).

This volume corrects the following typographical errors in the source texts, cited by page and line number: 46.11, lubricates; 48.3, seperate; 81.25, Tighten; 82.27 Soft-minded; 157.1, And; 164.28, 'To.

The following is a list of pages where a stanza break coincides with the foot of the page (except where such breaks are apparent from the regular stanzaic structure of the poem): 26, 39, 41, 45, 60, 62, 83, 103, 112, 133, 134, 152, 154, 156, 158, 159, 168, 178, 189, 190, 191, 201, 215.

NOTES

2.3   a month . . . cells]   Pound was confined at the army prison camp at Pisa from May 24 to June 15, 1945, in a cage made of wood and steel mesh that was similar to the ones used to hold condemned prisoners. He was moved to a tent in the medical compound after suffering an apparent mental breakdown.

2.7   Δρυάς]   Dryad.

2.7   Taishan]   Sacred mountain in West Shantung, China.

2.13   Chocorua]   A peak in the White Mountains, New Hampshire.

2.19   Plura diafana]   "More things diaphanous": from Robert Grosseteste (d. 1253), *Of Light*.

2.20   Heliads]   Daughters of Helios, changed into poplar trees while mourning their brother Phaëton.

2.22   *'udor*]   Water.

15.3–4   *'All too . . . 1944*]   "The Reverend James Gordon Gilkey, *The New York Times*, 7th June 1944." [Moore's note.]

23.8   Compiègne]   France surrendered to Germany at Compiègne on June 22, 1940.

23.18   Kimmel and Short]   Admiral Husband Edward Kimmel (1882–1968), commander of U.S. Pacific Fleet in 1941; Lieutenant General Walter Short (1880–1949), army commander in Hawaii in 1941. Both men were removed from their commands after the Japanese attack.

23.23   Brave Brooks and lithe MacLeish]   Van Wyck Brooks and Archibald MacLeish.

24.6   *The Irresponsibles*]   A book published in 1940 by Archibald MacLeish (then serving as Librarian of Congress), to which Tate's poem is a direct response. MacLeish's theme—the responsibility of intellectuals, American and European, in the fall of Europe—is sounded in his opening question: "Why did the scholars and writers of our generation in this country, witnesses as they were to the destruction of writing and of scholarship in great areas of Europe and to the exile and the imprisonment and murder of men whose crime was scholarship and writing . . . fail to oppose those forces while they could—while there was still time and still place to oppose them with the arms of scholarship writing?"

29.18–19   first bombs were fallen on Hellas]   Italy invaded Greece on October 28, 1940.

37.16   *restricted*]   Term used in American advertising for real estate and public accommodations during the 1940s to indicate that Jews were unwelcome.

41.18   Linz]   Hitler attended high school in Linz, Austria, from 1900 until 1904, when he was asked to leave, and then lived in the city from 1905 to 1908.

48.12–13   Bulfinch's golden dome]   The Massachusetts State House, built in 1795–98 by Charles Bulfinch.

49.1–2   when he slapped that soldier down]   The incident occurred in a hospital tent during the Sicilian campaign in 1943; Eisenhower subsequently forced Patton to apologize publicly.

50.23   SHAEF]   Supreme Headquarters Allied Expeditionary Force.

55.1   P.O.E.]   Port of Embarkation.

78.7   Phaëthon]   Son of Helios, the sun god; exacting from his reluctant father the boon of guiding the chariot of the sun for a single day, he lost control of the horses and was killed by Zeus in order to save the world from a disastrous conflagration.

86.8–10   Leopold . . . Begun]   Over the opposition of his cabinet, King Leopold III of Belgium surrendered unconditionally to Germany on May 28, 1940; in 1936, he had announced the abandonment of Belgium's alliance with France in favor of a policy of neutrality.

87.2   Eighth Air Force]   "EIGHTH AIR FORCE is a poem about the air force which bombed the Continent from England. The man who lies counting missions has one to go before being sent home. The phrases from the Gospels compare such criminals and scapegoats as these with that earlier criminal and scapegoat about whom the Gospels were written." [Jarrell's note.]

88.1   The Death . . . Gunner]   "A ball turret was a plexiglass sphere set into the belly of a B-17 or B-24, and inhabited by two .50 caliber machine-guns and one man, a short small man. When this gunner tracked with his machine-guns a fighter attacking his bomber from below, he revolved with the turret; hunched upside down in his little sphere, he looked like the foetus in the womb. The fighters who attacked him were armed with cannon firing explosive shells. The hose was a steam hose." [Jarrell's note.]

88.7   Transient Barracks]   "At one time in the Second Air Force—the bomber training command—one member of every bomber crew was ordered to learn to play the ocarina 'in order to improve the morale of the crew overseas.' It was strange to walk along a dark road and look up at the big desert stars and hear from the distant barracks a gunner playing his ocarina. The hero of TRANSIENT BARRACKS, after some years abroad as a gunner, is a gunnery instructor now. A *G.I. can* is what you and I would call a garbage can; a *'24* is a B-24, a Liberator, a bomber very like a truck. In a *day-room* soldiers spend their evenings shooting pool or listening to the radio, or writing home. When you shaved in the barracks you usually had the choice of a broken glass mirror in which you could recognize part of yourself, or a mirror of unbroken metal in which you could see a face. The *C.Q.* is the soldier in Charge of Quarters. Before a man left a field every department of the field had to sign a clearance saying that he had kept nothing of theirs—but as you see, everyone went away with something." [Jarrell's note.]

89.14   O My Name It Is Sam Hall]   "The men in *O My Name It is Sam Hall* are three American prisoners and one American M.P., at a B-29 training base in southern Arizona. The guard's song begins

> *O my name it is Sam Hall, it is Sam Hall.*
> *O my name it is Sam Hall, it is Sam Hall.*
> *O my name it is Sam Hall,*
> *And I hate you one and all—*
> *Yes, I hate you one and all,*
> *God damn your eyes.*" [Jarrell's note.]

90.13   A Camp in the Prussian Forest]   "An American soldier is speaking after the capture of one of the German death camps. Jews, under the Nazis, were made to wear a yellow star. The Star of David is set over Jewish graves as the Cross is set over Christian graves." [Jarrell's note.]

92.3–4   "*Yet these elegies . . . is warn.*"]   Cf. Wilfred Owen's preface for a planned volume of his poems: "My subject is War, and the pity of War. The Poetry is in the pity. Yet these elegies are to this generation in no sense consolatory. They may be to the next. All a poet can do today is warn. That is why true Poets must be truthful."

92.5–6   "*The old Lie: . . . Pro patria mori.*"]   Cf. "Dulce et Decorum." The Latin phrase, from Horace (*Odes* III, ii, 13), translates: "It is sweet and fitting to die for one's country."

95.5–6   Tokyo Rose]   Name applied to various women who broadcast in English on behalf of the Japanese government during World War II, but especially to Iva Toguri D'Aquino (b. 1916), an American citizen stranded in Japan at the outbreak of the war who in 1943 became the announcer for the propaganda program *Zero Hour.* She was convicted of treason in 1949 and sentenced to ten years. Released in 1956, she was pardoned by President Gerald Ford in 1977.

97.2   Bond Street Station]   A station in the London Underground.

101.19   *Angels one-two*]   Radio code for an altitude of 12,000 feet.

108.11   "*longen . . . pilgrimages*,"]   Cf. Geoffrey Chaucer, prologue to *The Canterbury Tales.*

109.17   Icarian]   Pertaining to Icarus, the son of the inventor Daedalus; escaping from imprisonment with his father by means of wax wings that the latter had made, he flew too close to the sun and was drowned in the Aegean Sea.

110.6   "*Vale*" from Carthage]   "The word 'vale' (Latin for 'farewell') was used on Roman tombstones. 'Ave atque vale' is, of course, the phrase immortalized by Catullus in his elegy to his brother, killed fighting for Rome in an older war than mine. As a sergeant in the U.S. Army's African campaign in March 1944, I was among the Roman tombstones in the ruins of Carthage when I heard the news that my brother was killed by a German bullet in the Anzio beachhead, near Rome. He and I had met last at Times Square, New York." [Viereck's note.]

111.11   Ripeness Is All]   *King Lear,* V.ii.11.

112.3   *Rejoice . . . youth*]   This and the other italicized phrases in the poem can be found in Ecclesiastes 11:8–9.

115.3   *Dorie Miller*]   Doris Miller (1919–43), who served as ship's cook, third class, on the battleship *West Virginia,* was awarded the Navy Cross for his actions during the Japanese attack on Pearl Harbor. He was killed in the sinking of the escort carrier *Liscome Bay* in the Gilbert Islands.

121.9   Lepke]   Louis "Lepke" Buchalter (1897–1944), New York labor racketeer and leader of the gang of hired killers popularly known as "Murder, Incorporated." Lepke was executed at Sing Sing prison in 1944.

122.5   West Street Jail]   Common name for the federal detention center in lower Manhattan that opened in 1929 and closed in 1975.

122.15   Bioff and Brown]   Willie Bioff and George Brown, Chicago gangsters who were convicted in 1941 of using their control of the film projectionists union to extort money from Hollywood studios.

126.11   Jackie Cooper]   Child star (b. 1922) in Hollywood movies of the '30s, including *The Champ* (1931) and *Peck's Bad Boy* (1934).

139.12   Acheron]   River in Greece which, in *The Odyssey* and elsewhere, is depicted as leading to the entrance to Hades.

142.5–6   *Per ardua . . . Per aspera,*]   Cf. "Per ardua ad astra" (Through adversity to the stars), motto of the Royal Air Force.

142.11 IFF] Identification Friend or Foe, a signaling device carried on aircraft for that purpose. [Nemerov's note.]

143.5 OTU] Operational Training Unit.

144.7 When Italy . . . day,] Italy invaded Ethiopia on October 3, 1935.

152.3–4 *Denke daran . . . war.*] "Think of this, that after the great destructions, every man will know that he was innocent." From the play *Träume* (Dreams, 1953).

152.5 *Or hast . . . God?*] Job 40:9.

164.21 B.A.R.] Browning Automatic Rifle.

165.17 Tyrtaeus] Poet and military leader (7th century B.C.) who led the Spartans in the Second Messenian War.

167.8–10 when Hera rallied . . . yelled from Stentor's mouth] Cf. *The Iliad*, Book V.

168.27–169.1 *"Gott mit uns"* . . . belts.] "God with us": the phrase was inscribed on the belt buckles of German soldiers.

169.22–23 "The Singing Horses of Buchenwald"] Name given by the SS to the prisoners, many of them Jewish, who were chained to carts and forced to sing while hauling stones out of the camp quarry.

169.25 *Die Vögelein . . . Walde,*] Cf. Goethe, "Wanderer's Night Song II": The little birds are silent in the woods.

170.13–14 *"I cried . . . bill."*] Psalm 3:4.

170.15 "More light! More light!"] Last words of Goethe, who died at his home in Weimar.

183.9 Carentan] Town in Normandy captured by American troops on June 11, 1944.

188.19 the Bloody Angle] Confederate position at Spotsylvania Court House, Virginia, captured by Union troops on May 12, 1864.

189.18–19 a Simone . . . Veronica.] Simone Simon, French film actress (b. 1910) who went to Hollywood and starred in *Cat People* (1942) and other films; Veronica Lake (1919–1973), whose films included *This Gun for Hire* (1942) and *So Proudly We Hail* (1943).

190.14 "Je t'attends toujours."] "I will wait for you forever."

206.4 Westbrook Pegler] Pegler (1894–1969) was a columnist for the New York *World-Telegram* and other newspapers.

ABOUT THIS SERIES

The American Poets Project offers, for the first time in our history, a compact national library of American poetry. Selected and introduced by distinguished poets and scholars, elegant in design and textually authoritative, the series will make widely available the full scope of our poetic heritage.

For other titles in the American Poets Project, or for information on subscribing to the series, please visit www.americanpoetsproject.org.

ABOUT THE PUBLISHER

The Library of America, a nonprofit publisher, is dedicated to preserving America's best and most significant writing in handsome, enduring volumes, featuring authoritative texts. For a free catalog, to subscribe to the series, or to learn how you can help support The Library's mission, please visit www.loa.org or write: The Library of America, 14 East 60th Street, New York, NY 10022.

AMERICAN POETS PROJECT

EDNA ST. VINCENT MILLAY: SELECTED POEMS
J. D. McClatchy, editor
ISBN 1-931082-35-9 $20.00

———

POETS OF WORLD WAR II
Harvey Shapiro, editor
ISBN 1-931082-33-2 $20.00

———

KARL SHAPIRO: SELECTED POEMS
John Updike, editor
ISBN 1-931082-34-0 $20.00

———

WALT WHITMAN: SELECTED POEMS
Harold Bloom, editor
ISBN 1-931082-32-4 $20.00